Table of Contents

Introduction

Before I start, I would like to say a few things about myself. This is because I am afraid, once you are done reading this book you might get a wrong impression about me. I would not blame you if you thought I am a staunch Democrat. In actuality, I am a registered independent who does not actively participate in the political process but one who keeps himself engaged on the issues being discussed and on the policies being proposed.

Instead of going to the political town hall meetings and asking questions to the politicians, I tend to yell at the TV (a lot). So, I am mostly a step or two removed from the mainstream political process.

I am an immigrant who migrated over 30 years ago. I have been an American citizen for more than 25 years and have participated in the electoral process ever since I became eligible to vote. I vote purely based on who I think is better for our country irrespective of which party they belong to. So, yes, I have voted for both Democrats and for Republicans over time. I am not a loyalist of either party; I am fiercely independent. I am socially and fiscally moderate and worry deeply about the national debt and the direction our country is headed. As such, I tend to side with the Democrats on some issues and side with the Republicans on others. So, one can say, I am truly on the fence – a real independent!

By the way, keep a watch out for the "Debunking the Democratic Myth" book coming out soon.

The idea about numbers, about math and about who is telling the truth started for me on September 5, 2012. This was the night when President Bill Clinton gave a speech at the 2012 Democratic Convention in Charlotte, NC.

Even though it was a long speech, as I listened to it several things stuck with me for a long time after the speech was over - especially his line about Arithmetic. He went on to explain how the Republican budgets over the years did not meet the basic math test - that two plus two equals four - and thus their budgets and policies were responsible for significant increases in deficits and debt. He gave several statistics to support his claim. For eg:

> He said that in the past 52 years (since 1961), the economy created 52 million jobs - 24 million under the Republicans and 42 million under the Democrats - almost double than the Republicans!

> He also mentioned that the budget deficit quadrupled under Republican administrations 12 years prior to him taking office. And then doubled again in the 8 years after he left office under Republicans.

When I heard these numbers, my first reaction was disbelief. I said to myself this couldn't be right. There must be something wrong with the stats the president is presenting. Because most of us have been led to believe that the Republicans are better stewards of the economy and that they are better at creating jobs and that they are better at managing the budget and the deficit. But Clinton was saying exactly opposite.

So, naturally my second reaction was suspicion. I was sure president Clinton was manipulating the numbers to better fit his narrative. But this time, instead of just listening to the numbers being thrown around by either party, I thought maybe I should spend some time and look at the numbers myself to see where the truth lies. So, I decided that I must investigate and find out for myself who is telling the truth. Thus started my quest to research the numbers to find the truth.

The more statistics I looked at the more I became convinced that Clinton was indeed right. I slowly began to realize that I had been brainwashed by the Republican rhetoric to such an extent that any contrary point of view or any contrary claim would immediately raise suspicion in my mind.

So as the truth began to dawn on me, I also began to wonder about one more thing. I wondered how many countless others, who like me, believe in this alternative Republican reality? As I was pondering about this, I figured since I have already done the research and compiled this data, why not share this with others?

It was at this point I decided to write this book - to share my research and to open people's eyes to the truth. For over four decades we have been listening to the rhetoric from the Republican Party and being brainwashed to believe in alternative reality - the only problem is that it is completely bogus, as the evidence will suggest.

As you read this book, I hope to convince you of the actual reality and hope that you, like me, will see the real truth in the numbers. Because, after all, the numbers do not lie.

Getting Started

When I got started with the research, initially I decided to focus only on the statistics that President Clinton talked about at the convention. This was because I really did not know what information was out there and I honestly was not thinking beyond this. All I was interested at that point was to see for myself if the points made by Clinton were true or not. So, that is what I focused on initially.

Right away I noticed something very peculiar. Normally, the Republican attack machine does not waste any time refuting anything negative that is said about them no matter if it is true or not. They immediately go on a coordinated counterattack and target the message and the messenger to discredit them. But, for some reason not this time. Indeed, there were a few reports here and there, some agreeing with what Clinton said and some disagreeing. However, over a period of several days, I had not seen or heard any coordinated attack other than a few bloggers here and there. It's possible they have done this, but I don't recall coming across any of this in the mainstream media, which I watch frequently. Did this mean they agreed with his figures? If not, why the silence, I wondered?

Anyway, off I went with my research. As I started to uncover the truth and started to realize that indeed Clinton was right (to what extent, we will see in later chapters), I began to wonder what other things that the Republicans were telling us that were also incorrect? It was then I thought I should expand my research and put together a more comprehensive narrative that includes a boarder analysis.

Even with the decision to expand the research, I still did not want to leave it open-ended. Therefore, I decided to focus on the Republican talking points and see if there is any truth in them.

The Republican rhetoric against Democrats broadly falls into the following categories:

1. Democrats create more government jobs than private sector jobs.

2. Democrats are big spenders and are mostly responsible for the deficits and the debt.

3. Democrats are for big government and are responsible for significant growth of the federal government.

4. Democrats are anti-business and support socialist policies over capitalistic free market based policies and are generally bad for the business.

5. Democrats spend, spend and spend on education and have nothing to show for it.

6. Democrats are for high taxes and redistribution of wealth from the rich to the poor.

7. Democrats are mostly "takers" and Republicans are mostly "makers".

In this book, I hope my research and the figures I present will either support the above claims by the Republicans against the Democrats or debunk them.

A word of caution: there is a lot of data out there for consumption. However, a lot of this data is not consistent. Sometimes data for one topic may be listed under other unrelated topics or sometimes what exactly is included in the data is not clear. Most of the data comes with caveats that are listed in fine print. And if one does not pay attention to these intricacies and nuances, one might inadvertently exclude some important data or make incorrect assumptions resulting in incorrect interpretations.

Therefore, any data presented here must be taken with a grain of salt. The intention here is not to present data as an exact science but as an approximation. For the purposes of this discussion, this approximation should not impact the overall analysis and interpretations presented here, as this analysis is high level in nature. If this is well understood, it should be fine. Also, I have included the source where I got the data from so it should be easy for anyone to get to this data and do their own research and analysis.

The chapters are organized based on the broad categories mentioned above. In the final chapter, I will summarize the narrative, which I hope will convince you in believing the alternative reality Republicans have painted for you. If you are still not convinced, or are still skeptical, I hope this book will at least convince you to do your own research and figure it out for yourselves.

It's Jobs, Jobs and Jobs

In his 2010 democratic convention address, Bill Clinton said, "...since 1961, for 52 years now, the Republicans have held the White House 28 years, the Democrats, 24. In those 52 years, our private economy has produced 66 million private sector jobs. So, what's the job score? Republicans, 24 million; Democrats, 42 (million)".

I created the following chart using non-farm employment data from the Bureau of Labor Statistics from the years 1961 to 2012. Non-farm employment data counts only those who are employed in the private sector. Importantly, this data does not include the unemployed, and government jobs.   Therefore, non-farm employment data is considered a better representative of the true private employment situation.   As can be seen from the chart, the non-farm jobs under the Democratic presidents were 43 million as opposed to 30 million under Republican presidents.

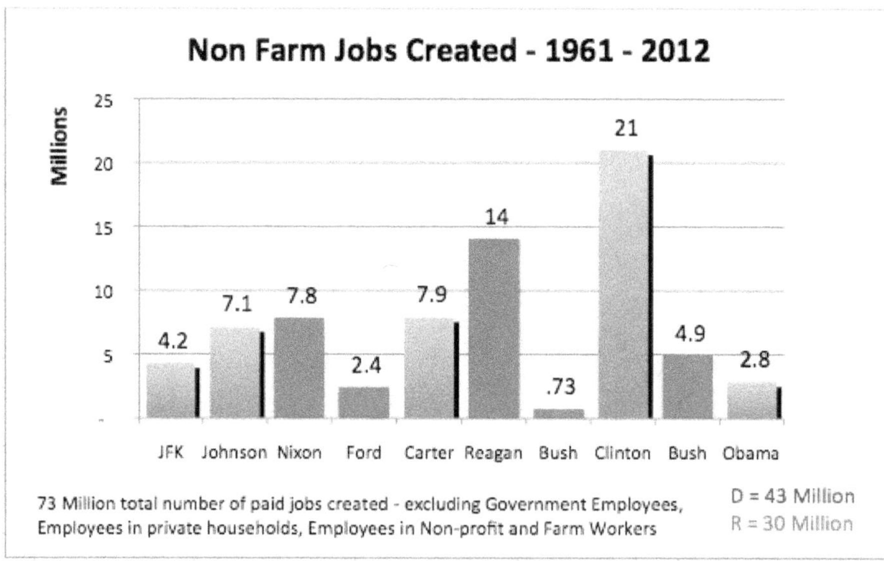

As you can tell, these numbers do not exactly match Clinton's numbers from the DNC speech. I am not sure which set of numbers Clinton used because I looked at data in different categories but none of it closely matched Clinton's. Right after his speech there were some blogs and news articles, some agreeing with Clinton's numbers and some refuting him.

Most notably, factcheck.org published an article titled "Our Clinton Nightmare" on September 6, 2012, in which they claimed that Clinton was mostly right. Another article on usnews.com dated Sep 6, 2012 tiled "Bill Clinton Is Right: The Economy Really Does Do Better Under Democrats", also confirmed that the numbers quoted by Clinton were right. In this article, Rick Newman goes on to say"… I crunched the numbers a few different ways to see if Clinton was cherry-picking the best numbers. His figures measure job gains from the month a president took office until the month he left. Since it takes a year or so for any president's policies to go into effect, I also measured job gains from one year after each president took office till one year after he left. Here's the score by that measure: Democrats: 38 million new jobs, Republicans, 27 million."

On May 8th 2012, an article in Bloomberg.com titled, "Private Jobs Increase More With Democrats in White House", also highlighted that more private sector jobs were created under the Democrats than under Republicans.

On the other side, Allen Ginzburg in a blog "Bill Clinton's DNC 2012 Speech: Good and Dishonest" dated September 6, 2012 writes "…More than half of the Democrat total here came from Clinton's Presidency. That presidency occurred during the innovative computer and Internet boom that almost automatically produced jobs. Furthermore, this ignores that during 6 out of 8 years of the Clinton Presidency; Republicans controlled Congress and set many of the nation's policies…"

That is a good observation I guess but I am not sure if this refutes the point Clinton was making. According to Mr. Ginzburg, the job creation under Clinton was only attributable to the Internet boom and to congress. It is true that there was an Internet boom, and the economy was doing well. But such good economic booms also occurred during Republican presidents as well. For eg: under Regan the economy was doing quite well. And yes, Republicans held both houses of congress during the last 6 years of Clinton's presidency and it is also true they introduced many bills. But if Clinton did not sign them, they would not have been implemented. So, either way one looks at it, Clinton was involved in the decision-making process and was ultimately responsible for the creation of jobs during his presidency. If he wanted to, Clinton could have vetoed many of these legislations since the Republicans did not have enough votes to override his veto.

Now, there is one interesting thing to note. He mentions that more than half of the jobs created under the Democratic presidents were created under Clinton. But he fails to mention that of the 30 million jobs created under Republican presidents over 14 million of these were created under Reagan's presidency. And guess who was in charge of congress during the Reagan presidency? The Democrats held the house all 8 years and the senate the last 2 years.

So, if we use Mr. Ginzburg's logic, then all the jobs created under Reagan's presidency should be attributable to the Democrats as they held the house all 8 years of his presidency. In fact, if we are to use Mr. Ginzburg's logic, job creation in general should be attributable to the congress and not the presidents. So, why do we always hold the presidents accountable for job creation?

Anyway, back to the discrepancy between the numbers between what Clinton quoted and what I have shown above. The main reason for this discrepancy might be related to which historical data Clinton was using. The Bureau of Labor Statistics (BLS) publishes several different historical tables. For eg: it publishes **Civilian Labor Force** statistics, **Civilian Employment** statistics and **Total Non Farm Employment** statistics all of which are available as seasonal adjusted or unadjusted. Each of these data tables includes different components of the labor force. For eg: the Civilian labor force includes all persons in the civilian non-institutional population either employed or ***unemployed***, whereas the Non-Farm Labor statistics include jobs in the private sector plus all civilian government jobs (excluding active military personnel and farm labor).

As mentioned earlier, I used the Non-Farm Labor statistics, as it did not make sense to use the job statistics that included the unemployed population when one is trying to determine how many jobs were created under each president. In addition to excluding the unemployed, the Non-Farm statistics also excludes employees in private households and the employees working in non-profit and employees who volunteer and uniformed military personnel.

Also, I took a slightly different approach than what some suspect Clinton did. Instead of measuring the job growth from the month the president took office, I measured the job gains (or losses) from the ***year*** a president was sworn in to the last full year he was in office. For instance, in the case of Clinton, my analysis attributed the job gains/losses to Clinton for the entire year of 1993 and the entire year of 2000 (end of his second term) even though he took oath for his first term in Feb 1993 and ended his second term in Feb 2001. So, technically Bush (senior) would have been responsible for Jan 2009, but as I mentioned earlier, my analysis is an approximation and not an exact up to a single job scientific analysis. Therefore, to keep things simple, I used the year in which the president was sworn in instead of the month.

As the graph on the previous page shows, even using the Non Farm Labor statistics (which excludes the unemployed), it appears the Democrats are ahead in the job count – 43 million to 30 million jobs.

So, Clinton was somewhat correct about the creation of private sector jobs.

Now, here's another statistic related to government job creation that is interesting. In the Bloomberg article mentioned earlier, it is noted that "... Since January 1961, federal, state and local government employment grew by 7.1 million under Republican presidents and 6.3 million when Democrats were in the White House."

So, basically 800,000 more "government sector" jobs (which include federal, state and local government jobs) were created under **Republican** presidents than during the Democratic presidents! Interesting.

The article also shows that if one looks at *federal agency jobs* alone, the Republicans added 21,000 jobs per month v/s Democrats 22,000 jobs per month. Thus, over the period of 51 years, the Republicans added about 12.8 million federal agency jobs and the Democrats added 13.4 million jobs. This comes out to Democrats adding about 600,000 more federal jobs than Republicans over a period of 51 years (about 5% more).

Now, ask yourself this. Is this number that dramatically different from the Republicans? Yes it is higher, but is a difference of 600,000 jobs over 51 years out of a total 26 million jobs created that *significantly* different to support the Republican narrative that Democrats are the only ones responsible for bigger government.

The Republicans say they are for smaller government. In fact,

Reagan started the "government is the problem" revolution. But, despite this constant drumbeat from the Republicans, it appears that both parties have almost equally contributed to the growth of federal government jobs over the years.

But, as we have seen above, on the private sector side, the Democrats beat the Republicans hands down. On the government sector jobs, which include federal, state and local government jobs, Republicans added 7.1million jobs v/s Democrats 6.3million. If one looks at federal jobs alone, Democrats have added about 800,000 jobs more than Republicans over the past 51years (less than 5% more) – not significantly more than Republicans. So, I would like to think this myth is debunked.

Deficit and Debt

At the 2012 convention, president Clinton also said the following about the deficit and the national debt....”...Don't you ever forget when you hear them talking about this that Republican economic policies quadrupled the national debt before I took office, in the 12 years before I took office and doubled the debt in the eight years after I left, because it defied arithmetic. It was a highly inconvenient thing for them in our debates that I was just a country boy from Arkansas, and I came from a place where people still thought two and two was four. It's arithmetic.”

According to Clinton, for 12 years before he was sworn in, the Republicans quadrupled the national debt and doubled the debt again in the next 8 years after he left and blew away the surplus that Clinton created. Let's see how the numbers stack up. The table below shows the national debt from 1977 to 2010. It also includes which president was in office and what party he belonged to.

Year	Debt (millions)	% of GDP	President	Party	Year	Debt (millions)	% of GDP	President	Party
1977	706,398	35.8	Carter	D	1995	4,920,586	67.0	Clinton	D
1978	776,602	35.0	Carter	D	1996	5,181,465	67.1	Clinton	D
1979	829,467	33.2	Carter	D	1997	5,369,206	65.4	Clinton	D
1980	909,041	33.4	Carter	D	1998	5,478,189	63.2	Clinton	D
1981	994,828	32.5	Reagan	R	1999	5,605,523	60.9	Clinton	D
1982	1,137,315	35.3	Reagan	R	2000	5,628,700	57.3	Clinton	D
1983	1,371,660	39.9	Reagan	R	2001	5,769,881	56.4	Bush	R
1984	1,564,586	40.7	Reagan	R	2002	6,198,401	58.8	Bush	R
1985	1,817,423	43.8	Reagan	R	2003	6,760,014	61.6	Bush	R
1986	2,120,501	48.2	Reagan	R	2004	7,354,657	63.0	Bush	R
1987	2,345,956	50.4	Reagan	R	2005	7,905,300	63.6	Bush	R
1988	2,601,104	51.9	Reagan	R	2006	8,451,350	64.0	Bush	R
1989	2,867,800	53.1	Bush	R	2007	8,950,744	64.6	Bush	R
1990	3,206,290	55.9	Bush	R	2008	9,986,082	69.7	Bush	R
1991	3,598,178	60.7	Bush	R	2009	11,875,851	85.1	Obama	D
1992	4,001,787	64.1	Bush	R	2010	13,528,807	94.3	Obama	D
1993	4,351,044	66.1	Clinton	D	2011	14,025,215	98.6	Obama	D
1994	4,643,307	66.6	Clinton	D	2012	16,050,921	103.2	Obama	D
					2011	14,764,222	98.9	Obama	D
					2012	16,050,921	103.2	Obama	D

As can be seen from the table, the year when Carter left office (1980), the national debt was $909 billion at 33.4% of GDP. In the year when Clinton took office (1993), the national debt stood at $4.3 trillion at 66% of GDP.   The debt went from $909 billion to $4.3 trillion.... basically, quadrupled during the Reagan years! This confirms what Clinton said in his speech.

Now let's see what happened in the eight years after Clinton left office. The debt was at $5.6 trillion when Clinton left office in 2000 at 57% of GDP (yes, that's right!   The debt as a % of GDP went down under Clinton - from 66% to 57% even though the debt in dollars went up).

When George W Bush left office in 2008, the debt was at $9.9 trillion. This is not almost double from when Clinton left office, but close.   Clinton in his speech was off by $1.6 trillion. Nevertheless, the debt did increase from $5.6 trillion to $9.9 trillion (a 76% increase!) under George W. and that is quite significant indeed. Please keep a note of the 76% increase in debt under George W as we will compare this to Obama shortly.

Note: if you look at the table above it shows that Clinton added 1.6 trillion to the overall debt.   This is true. However, the GDP% of the debt went down (to 57%) because the revenues went up (overall economy under Clinton did very well and tax increases brought in higher revenues). Therefore, the debt to GDP ratio comes out favorably. Also note that even though Clinton did eliminate the budget deficit during the last 4 years of his term, the debt continued to increase due to accounting gimmicks. Clinton used the excess money flowing into Social Security as government income, which reduced the budget deficit but did not actually help in paying down the debt.

Now let's take a broader look at the national debt instead of just the few years prior and a few years after Clinton. Let's look at how the deficit fared under each of the presidents from JFK to Obama (over a 51-year period).   The graph below shows the *addition* to the national debt by the respective presidents from 1961 thru 2012.

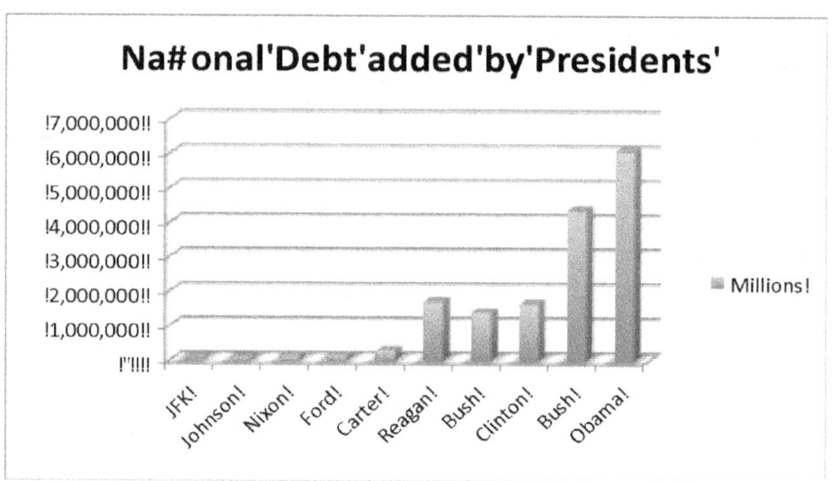

As can be clearly seen, the increase in debt started climbing significantly during the Reagan presidency and continued to climb since then.   Basically, in the past 31 years - from 1981 (when Reagan took office) to the end of 2012 (end of Obama's first term) - over $15 trillion was added to the national debt!

Since the debt at the end of 2012 was about $16 trillion, this means over 90% of the national debt was added since Reagan! And most of it - over $10 trillion - was added just in the past 12 years between Bush W and Obama!!

Guess what happened since Reagan? Tax cuts!

Obviously, the debt under Obama increased significantly - there is no hiding it.   Under Bush W it went up by $4.3 trillion (in 8 years) and under Obama it went up by $6.06 trillion (in the first 4 years). A lot of conservatives focus on this fact and assert that this is directly due to the failed policies of Obama and his inability to control the deficit. There is no doubt Obama could have done better - perhaps he should have focused on fixing the economy as a higher priority rather than taking on health care or focusing on other priorities.

But, more importantly, we should look at the ***trend***. If one looks at the numbers closely, one begins to see a different story. For eg: the table below shows the growth of debt under George W. Bush year over year from 2001 thru 2008.

Debt Increase by George W and Obama	
Year	Debt Growth
2001 – W	141,181
2002 – W	428,520
2003 – W	561,613
2004 – W	594,643
2005 – W	550,643
2006 – W	546,050
2007 – W	499,394
2008 – W	1,035,338
2009 – O	1,889,769
2010 – O	1,652,956
2011 – O	1,235,415
2012 - O	1,286,699

There is obviously a steady growth in debt year over year in the beginning, but in the last year (2008) there is a significant jump in the growth of debt - almost double that of previous years. It went from $499 billion in 2007 to over $1 trillion in 2008. I am sure we all can remember the financial crisis of 2008 and can understand why. In 2008, the economy was losing over 750K jobs per month, hiring was at a standstill and the GDP shrank. And to top all this, in the second half of the year there was the banking crisis - several banks and major investment banks went bankrupt or got sold for pennies on the dollar just to survive. So, one can understand why there was a significant increase in debt - there was not enough revenue coming into the treasury.

(By the way, the increase in debt from $141 billion in 2001 to $428 billion in 2002, even though significant, may be attributed to the increase in spending after the attacks on September 11, 2001).

Now look at the table again and look at the first four years of Obama. The important thing to note here is the ***trend***. As we have seen above, over the initial 7 years under George W, the debt increase was pretty steady year over year. However, in 2008, the trend went off the chart.

And guess what? This increase in trend *continued* under Obama in the first few years. Obviously, the economic collapse which started late in 2008 and the resulting increase in debt, continued under Obama. This point is very important, so I will state it again.

Understanding the debt increase trend is very important. The trend in the initial years under George W was flat...and in the last year of his presidency it doubled. This indicates that the economy got progressively worse in the last couple of years and fell into a ditch in 2008 (which we all know it did). And most of this occurred during the last months of 2008. This means that when Obama took office in Feb 2009, the economy was in a significant ***downward trend*** (spiral). No president, neither Obama nor anyone else, could have reversed this trend immediately coming into the office or even several years after coming into office.

No one could have taken a ***trend*** that doubled the debt increase in the one year and reduced it significantly the very next year even under normal circumstances, leave alone under the economic situation Obama found himself in when he took office. And guess what? Obama could not reduce costs by cutting government spending. Because anything he did to cut spending would have made the economy even worse. In fact, he had to increase government spending to pump money into the economy to keep it from falling into a depression. Which of course increased the debt even more.

Now, let's try an experiment. Close your eyes again and go back to the last 5 months in 2008. I know, no one wants to re-live this, but please take this journey anyway; I am trying to make a point.

You should find yourself in the middle of a financial crisis. Over the past several months you have seen nothing but bad economic news all around – people being laid off everywhere, people unable to find jobs for months/years, housing prices down the sink hole. New home construction? Non-existent. You want to take out a loan? Good luck with that. Have you looked at your investments and your 401K lately? Depressing, isn't it? And of course, the housing market was already in the ditch by now with foreclosures on the rise and millions of homeowners' upside down on their mortgages.

Even with all this mess going around, I bet nothing prepared you for what is about to hit you. Starting in July/August 2008, we got hit with the "liquidity crisis". Basically, commercial banks and investment banks stopped trusting each other and nobody wanted to lend to anyone (even between banks) which perpetuated a complete shutdown of the banking system and caused several major institutions to fail or be bailed out (remember Lehman Brothers? AIG?). We were told the US economy - heck, the entire global economy - would not exist if things go further down the sinkhole. Everyone was on pins-and-needles wondering what was going to happen next. Remember that?

Remember also that all this happened barely 5 months before Obama came into office. Now, put yourself in Obama's position. You are the newly elected president about to take office and everything around you is falling apart. The economy is losing about a million jobs a month. Unemployment is around 12% (or whatever it was back then). Banks are failing left and right (according to FDIC, 140 banks failed in 2009 and 157 in 2010). Lending is non-existent - banks are not lending to each other or to other businesses. Mortgage lending does not exist. Housing market is in a complete collapse. Auto industry is in the tank and about to go bust.

And oh, I almost forgot, there are two major wars going on - Iraq and Afghanistan - and every day soldiers are coming home wounded or in body bags.

And another thing I forgot to add - there are nasty buggers out there trying to kill Americans every opportunity they get.

And there are a bunch of so-called patriotic Americans who have just decided they would do whatever they can to oppose any solution Obama put forth (yes, the Republicans in congress).

Are you with me so far? What would you have done? Under this circumstance, would reducing the deficit and reducing the debt be the first thing on our mind? Should reducing the debt even be a priority with everything else going around? What do you think?

And by the way, the option to reduce government spending did not even exist for you as a president. Why? Because layoffs from the government or cutting back on expenses during an economic collapse makes things worse. Most everyone (reasonable ones, that is) agree that during recession or near total collapse of the economy, government spending should increase even if it results in an increase in overall debt. Once the economy starts getting better, the debt can be dealt with. In fact, John Keynes put forth the idea that the government should increase spending during economic downturns at the risk of increase in debt. And Republicans believe in this philosophy religiously.

The Obama administration rightly focused on stopping the job slide - they passed a stimulus plan and bailed out companies and extended unemployment payments, extended welfare benefits etc., all of which were geared towards pumping money into the economy and stopping the slide of the economy going deeper into the rat-hole. Now, whether some of these programs were effectively executed is a whole different story and not part of the scope of this book, but they did indeed help reverse the trend somewhat.

Of course, all this did not help with reducing the debt. In fact, it put it on a higher trajectory. But what choice would anyone have? The timing of the financial disaster occurred at a very unfortunate time for Obama and a most opportune time for Bush - just as he was getting out. I wonder how George W would have handled it if this financial mess occurred in 2004 or 2005 with both the wars raging on? Would he have focused on reducing the deficit and debt or would he have focused first on fixing the economy? And would the Republicans have made the same amount of noise as they are making now?

If you took another look at the previous table, you would also notice that the debt increases in 2011 and 2012 went down from 2010 (from $1.65 trillion in 2010 to $1.28 trillion in 2012). So, the trend has been turned around. Some of this is due to tax increases passed recently but mostly due to the economy getting better and generating more revenue into the treasury coffers. This is the normal cycle in any recession….it takes some time to reverse the trend. And as I have stated above, from a timing point of view, the change in administrations between George W and Obama occurred at a time when the major impact of the worst recession in our history was just being felt when Obama took over.

Before we move on to the next chapter, let's look at one more statistic. Some people may suggest that the statistics quoted by Clinton during the 2012 democratic convention were only a small snapshot in time (12 years prior and 8 years after him taking office), taken to substantiate the narrative Clinton was providing.

This is a fair point.

So, let's look at the national debt numbers from a wider perspective. Let's look at this from 1961 to 2012 (we could go beyond 1961, but anything beyond that is so insignificant that it hardly matters). As you can see below, the total contribution to the national debt by Democratic presidents from 1961 to 2012 is about $8 trillion.   The contribution to debt by the Republican presidents is $7.7 trillion. A difference of about $300 billion over 51 years!

National debt added since 1961 to 2012	
Party	Debt
Democrats	8,047,860
Republicans	7,710,413

So, is this what the conservatives complain about? Is this what makes Democrats big spenders? A mere $6 billion per year! Honestly, this does not even qualify as a rounding error when compared to the overall GDP of $16 trillion.

The bottom line is both the Democrats and the Republicans spent recklessly and have significantly contributed to the overall national debt. The only difference maybe is in what they spend at. This we will cover in the next chapter.

But, before we do that, let's look at one more statistic. Allow me to debunk one more Republican claim – the claim that Obama is the worst spender since God knows when.

An article in Forbes, points out that Obama actually spends the least of all the recent presidents. It goes on to say, "…It's enough to make even the most ardent Obama cynic scratch his head in confusion." It continues, "…Amidst all the cries of Barack Obama being the most prolific big government spender the nation has ever suffered, Marketwatch is reporting that our president has actually been tighter with a buck than any United States president since Dwight D. Eisenhower. Who knew?"

As the chart on the next page shows, Reagan and both Bush I & II were among the highest spenders, followed by Clinton.

It's the Republican propaganda that managed to convince some Americans that Obama is a big spender. They point to the dramatic growth in spending in 2009 as an example. But, as we have seen in the previous chapters, the increase in spending in 2009 is attributable more to the economic mess started in mid-year 2008 under Bush than to Obama. So, it turns out Obama is the least spender of all the previous presidents since Reagan. It is indeed enough to scratch your head in confusion, isn't it?

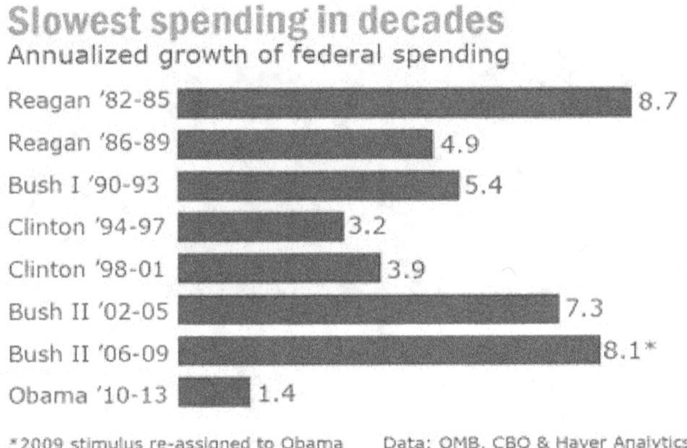

And of course, Obama took over a legacy which started two wars but did not pay for them, gave big tax cuts but did not pay for them, introduced a prescription drug plan but did not pay for it, introduced No Child Left Behind, but did not adequately fund it, and of course the worst economic crisis since the Great Depression. If you think about it, it's amazing that it only took Obama a couple of years to stop the car from going in the wrong direction and turn it around. As I mentioned before, the growth of spending was on the decline since 2010 and is projected to fall 1.3% in 2013.

As we have seen, both parties are responsible for increasing the national deficit and both parties are responsible for the growth of national debt.

So, another myth debunked.

So, *what* do they spend on and *how*?

In the last chapter we debunked the notion that Democrats are the only big spenders. We have noted that both parties contributed almost equally to the national debt since 1961. So, with all this spending going on, I began to wonder what it is that they are spending on? Is there a difference between the Democrats and the Republicans in what they spend money on? And is there a difference between how they spend?

Looks like there clearly is. Basically, Democrats spend money on programs that serve people mostly on the lower rung of the economic ladder including the elderly, the poor, the disabled, the unemployed and single mothers, the minorities and on those stuck in temporary unfortunate situations.

The Republicans also spend money; but their policies mostly benefit those on the higher income levels - mostly people that pay taxes, and mostly businesses. These differences arise because of their different belief systems, different values and different priorities.

But even more than this, another fundamental difference is in how they **account** for it.

But, before we go into this, allow me to digress a little bit and provide a brief background. In general, the federal government spends its money using three categories – Mandatory Spending, Discretionary Spending and Interest Payments. Mandatory spending comprises most of the federal spending (57% in 2012), followed by Discretionary spending (36% in 2012) and lastly Interest payments (6% in 2012 - see chart below).

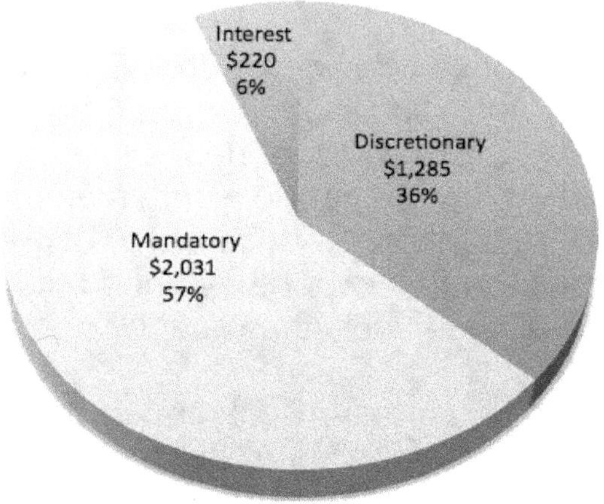

Mandatory spending includes Social Security, Medicare, Medicaid, Income Security, Retirement Benefits, Veterans benefits, Supplemental Nutrition, Earned Income Child Credits, Disability and other programs, which in 2012 totaled $2.02-trillion – see chart below.

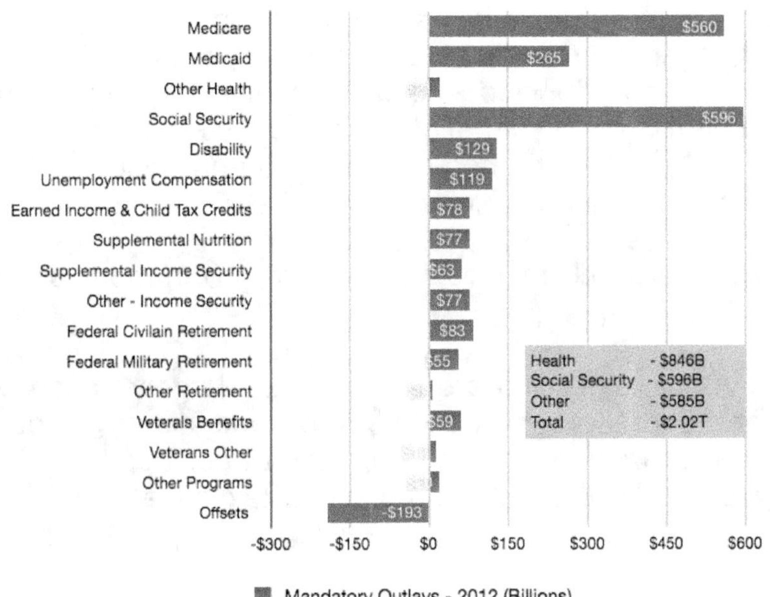

Mandatory Outlays - 2012 (Billions)

Discretionary spending on the other hand includes Defense and Education, Training, Transportation, Justice etc, which in 2012 totaled about $1.3-trillion (see chart below).

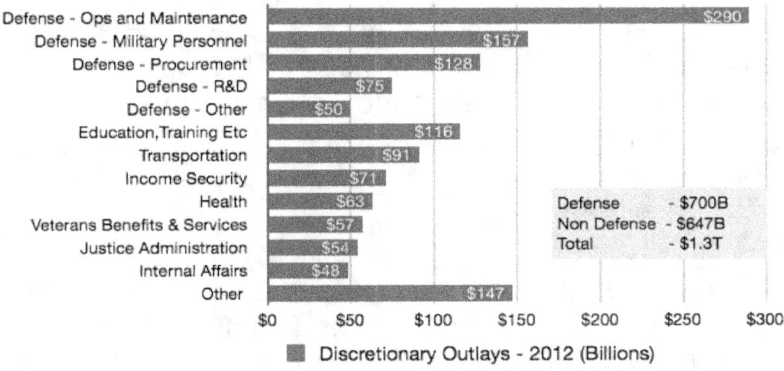

Discretionary Outlays - 2012 (Billions)

American **social spending** is generally called "entitlements" spending and mostly falls into the Mandatory category. Within this they are broken down into what some call ***social insurance*** programs and ***public assistance*** (or social welfare) programs. Social Insurance programs are contributory in nature, i.e. people pay into these and include Social Security, Disability, Medicare, and Unemployment benefits. Public Assistance (or social welfare) programs are non-contributory and include Medicaid, Feed Stamps, Extended unemployment etc.

OK. Let's get back to how the federal government spends or accounts for its spending.

American social policies are implemented largely based on two types are federal programs. One that works directly through the federal budget using what is known as Direct Spending and the other that works indirectly through the tax code known as Tax Expenditures.

So, what is the difference between the two? From a social policy perspective, a simple way to look at it is that, under Direct Spending, you get something from the government (a check or a benefit). Under Tax Expenditure, you pay less to the government (in taxes).

This simple difference makes all the difference in the world between the policies of Democrats and Republicans and more importantly between the perception over which party is doing a better job handling the deficit and the debt. Equally important, this difference accounts for the different belief system between liberals and conservatives.

Direct Spending includes both Mandatory and Discretionary Spending, which as we have seen before, includes social benefits as well as defense, transportation and other spending and shows up on the books of the government from an accounting point of view – basically everything we have seen above.

Tax Expenditures on the other hand use a different accounting scheme that is considered "stealth" which allows the government to "spend", but this spending does not show up under its normal budget.

Tax Expenditures are programs designed to lower the tax liability of individuals and businesses by providing various programs including:

1. Tax Exclusions – allows one to exclude or exempt income from certain items from their gross income (e.g.: Foreign Income Tax Exclusion, Employer sponsored health insurance (a major item) etc).

2. Deductions – allows one to deduct items from the gross income or from taxable income (e.g.: home mortgage deduction, property tax deduction etc.).

3. Tax Grants – allows preferential tax rates for certain type of incomes (mostly educational. For instance, scholarship grants or Pell grants).

4. Tax Credits – allows one to apply credits directly to the tax liability (e.g.: child and dependent care credit, earned income tax credit, electric vehicle credit etc). Note: tax credits directly reduce one's tax liability whereas the deductions and exclusions and deferrals reduce the taxable income.

5. Tax Deferrals – allows one to defer taxes into the future for certain types of income (e.g.: payments into retirement savings plans (401K) are allowed pre-tax (up to a certain limit). Likewise, if one sells their home and buys another more expensive than the one they sold, any taxes on the capital gains on the home they just sold can be rolled into the new one (i.e.: deferred into the future). This deferral on the capital gains has a major loophole, which we will cover later.

Direct spending is easy to understand – these have clear visibility and show up on the government books and are discussed in the political arena every year during budget times.

Tax expenditures, on the other hand, are more nuanced because they are tax breaks. However, most people agree that they are government spending "disguised" as tax breaks. On face value they appear to be justifiable but look closely and you see a whole different story. This nuance with tax breaks (or deception as some would call it) plays into how these are perceived by the public depending on their philosophical viewpoint.

Allow me to explain. If one looks at the budget equation: Deficit or Surplus is equal to Revenue minus Spend (Deficit/Surplus = Revenue - Spend).

This should be obvious. If one spends more than one receives, one is in deficit. If one spends less than one receives, one is in surplus. Simple math.

The Direct Spending, we have seen so far obviously fall on the spend side of this equation. Tax Expenditures on the other hand **reduce** the revenues the government gets. But, because the reduction is calculated prior to the government receiving the revenue, they do not show up on the normal budget calculation. All one can see is that revenues were lower, but one does not have the visibility into **why** they were lower. Whereas, on the spend side one can clearly see where the dollars are being spent.

This is an important point so I would like to use an example and try to re-state it. Let's say you operate a store and the revenues for the month are $100 (let's keep it simple) and the expenses are $100. So, basically you are breaking even. Now let's say you paid $10 more a month for the telephone bill but your revenue remained the same. You now have a deficit of $10 (revenue = 100, expenses = 110). Anyone looking at your books can clearly see that the expenses went up and you have a deficit. Now let's take a different scenario. Instead of an increase in telephone bill, let's say you gave one of your customers a $10 discount. In this case, even though your expenses remained the same ($100), your revenue went down to $90. Therefore, you are still in a $10 deficit.

If anyone looks at your books, they can clearly see that revenue was down due to the discount you gave. Not so with the government budget. The tax expenditures are not recorded on the government books from a budget point of view. Therefore, these don't get noticed nor get debated on a frequent basis like the direct spending. Thus, they are known by their "stealth" moniker.

This difference in how the government "spends" and how the tax policies and spending policies are drafted arise from the philosophical differences between liberals and the conservatives. Let me provide another scenario.

Let's say you receive a tax deduction for $10,000 for the interest paid on your mortgage on your tax return. And let's say this deduction resulted in you paying $1,000 less in taxes. Now, would you consider the $1,000 you saved on your taxes a tax break or an entitlement? Like most Americans, you probably said of course this is a tax break and not an entitlement.

Your response to the above question may highlight this philosophical difference in perception related to Tax Expenditures (tax breaks) v/s Entitlement. If you understand this, you understand the gist of the problem.

Some people think getting a tax break does not amount to spending by the government (i.e.: entitlement) because this money never belonged to the government in the first place. You worked hard for it, you earned it and it's yours! You are simply keeping more of what you earned and sending less to the government.   Therefore, this should not constitute what the government considers its income and as such it cannot spend what did not belong to it to begin with and thus it is not an entitlement (i.e.: government spending).

Those on the other side think like this: it makes no difference if you are keeping the money (as a deduction) or getting a benefit from the government. It is still spending as far as the government is concerned, because this money is something you **would have owed** if it weren't for the deduction. Thus the government is getting less in revenue and it therefore jacks up the deficit side of the equation (recall the discount scenario from the store example above).

Let's look at this slightly differently. Let's say the mortgage interest deduction did not exist. Instead, assume it was implemented using the Direct Spending method. In this case, you would not have the mortgage interest deduction and would be required to pay all the taxes that were due. That is you paid $1,000 more in taxes as you could not take the $10,000 mortgage interest deduction. But, suppose the government turned around and sent you a check for $1,000 just because you paid mortgage interest. Now, in this scenario, would you consider this check from the government a benefit from the government or a tax break?

Again, your philosophical perspective may drive your response to the above question. But would you agree in this case the government is out of this revenue? The important difference in this scenario from the previous one is that, in this case, the government received extra revenue ($1K) and spent extra ($1K) both of which are clearly visible on its books.

Besides this nuanced difference, there is another major difference between tax expenditures and entitlement spending. What really irks the conservatives the most is the fact that the government sends checks (or provides benefits) to some people even though they have not paid any taxes.

This is the most controversial part of this whole discussion. It's one thing when the government sends you a check from what you paid (e.g.: Social Security, Unemployment, Medicaid etc.) or allows you to take a deduction up front from what you owe, but sending a check or providing a benefit to someone who had not paid any taxes? Now that's robbing Peter to pay Paul! And most people relate to this and think this is unfair.

But, from the liberal side, this is where the fairness doctrine, equal opportunity and the social policy issues come in. The liberals tend to value equal opportunity and fairness and what is good for the society in general and less so individualism.

The liberals contend that there are many unfair advantages dealt out to some citizens. For e.g.:

a. Why is it fair that someone who owes a mortgage is allowed to take a mortgage interest deduction and therefore pays less in taxes than someone who is renting an apartment is **not** allowed to deduct the rent and thus reduce their taxes? Why is this person, who presumably cannot afford to buy a home, but pays rent, penalized over someone who can afford to buy but pays less in taxes due to mortgage deductions?

Some might argue that the mortgage interest deduction was created to **encourage** home ownership and since home ownership is good for the overall economy, this deduction should not be considered an entitlement. If this is so, wouldn't it also be better to let renters deduct their rent payments so they could save to buy homes?

Or, why is it fair for the tax policies to allow someone to deduct the mortgage interest for a second home typically used as a vacation home (provided both mortgages are under $1 million) when those who don't own a second home cannot? Likewise, is it fair for anyone who owns a home to deduct interest on a home equity loan for up to $100,000 when those who don't own a home don't get such deductions? And mind you, home equity loans have nothing to do with encouraging homeownership – as we have seen recently, this only seems to encourage more spending and getting into bigger debt.

b. Why is it fair for some tax policies that allow someone like Romney to pay 14% in taxes on income of $13+ million simply because he earned most of his income from interest payments and dividends? Romney still avails himself of everything this country has to offer, infrastructure, business opportunities, laws and regulations, culture etc, so why is he allowed to pay less than others?

As you can see these are not easy questions to answer one-way or the other. You may lean towards one or the other depending on your philosophical view.

Which brings us to another confusing part about Direct Spending. As mentioned before, direct spending also includes Medicare and Social Security, which in fact make up over 57% of all federal direct spending. Even though the government is providing a benefit, most people believe these programs are not entitlements because people actually contribute to these through payroll taxes such as FICA (Social Security) at 12.4% (up to an income limit of $113,700 in 2013) and Medicare at 2.9%. The FICA and Medicare taxes are usually paid by employers and employees half and half. So, generally the employer pays 7.65% and the employee pays 7.65% up to the income limit.

Social Security, as you may know, was created to provide economic security to the retired, the disabled, or families of retired, disabled or deceased workers. It does this by collecting taxes (FICA) from workers throughout their working period and pays out Social Security benefits once they retire or get disabled. Because of Social Security, it is estimated that over 40% of retirees over 65 years and above are out of poverty.

Medicare, the other program along with Social Security, provides retirees aged 65 years and above or the disabled or those with serious medical conditions, federal health insurance program. The 2.9% of your income in taxes (half by you and half by your employer) paid throughout your working career pays for this benefit.

As mentioned above, most people do not think of Social Security and Medicare health insurance as entitlements. They view these as simply return on investments (contributions) they have been making throughout their working life. Whether or not people get back what they put in or they get a lot more than what they will be discussed in another chapter.

The contributions from employers and employees for Social Security and Medicare etc are indeed included in the revenue side of the equation. However, over the past few decades the spend side of these programs has increased more than the revenue side. Thus, these programs are contributing significantly to the budget deficit calculations. This will be covered more in another chapter.

The rhetoric from Republicans has been that entitlements are out of control and will bankrupt the country soon if they are not kept in check. Over the past several decades, the conservatives have done a masterful job in redefining entitlements into a much narrower definition relating to safety net (welfare) benefits. Starting with Reagan and his infamous "Welfare Queen" label, and to referring to Obama as the "Food Stamp President", these labels twisted these programs into pejorative terms.

The reality is that safety net programs (ie: welfare) programs cost around 9% of the federal spending. The majority of the spending is for Social Security, medical programs (Medicare, Medicaid, Children's health programs etc) and Defense and Interest payments. These contribute to about 72% of the total government spending.

One thing to note is that the Tax Expenditures also help low income earners. For example, the expanded use of the earned income tax credit and the child tax credits has also contributed towards driving up the Tax Expenditures. However, some say this was a "throw-in" or a "compromise" by the Republicans to get the Democrats to agree to the tax breaks for the rich.

Based on what we have seen above, from a social policy perspective, the liberals contend that the role of the government is to assist those in need and thus their policies shift income to the public sector where it is the government's role to help those that need it.

The conservative policies on the other hand, shift public funds to private markets where, they believe, the free markets are better suited to solve social issues or to individuals who they believe are better suited to solve their own problems.

This debate about social policies and fairness can go on and on with each side coming up with logical arguments to support their point of view. However, one thing is for sure, the Tax Expenditures for the most part shift the benefits to the high earners (most reasonable people agree on this).

That is why the liberals contend that the Tax Expenditures are nothing but government spending "masquerading" as tax breaks and therefore they don't get the visibility and the scrutiny they deserve. And importantly, from a political standpoint, it's easy for a politician to say they are for tax cuts rather than to say they are for spending - even though in this case both are effectively doing the same thing by reducing the revenue available to the government.

According to some economists, because Tax Expenditures operate essentially like Direct Spending, they have a significant impact on the budget due to loss in revenue. But because they are not readily identifiable in the budget, they are less transparent. And because they are less transparent, the general public does not focus on them but zoom in on the welfare components of the entitlement programs, which are very transparent and have great visibility (and of course, conservatives gladly point them out every opportunity they get).

Republicans took full advantage of this Tax Expenditures "loophole" and were able to pass many tax policies "under the radar" over the years and have shifted the wealth towards the higher earners. They also provided many tax breaks or loopholes to businesses.

How big a problem is this?   According to many sources, the Tax Expenditures account for anywhere from $1trillion to $1.2trillion per year in loss of federal revenue. That's over 25% of total government spend per year. In fact, Tax Expenditures "costs" more than Medicare and Medicaid combined (see the chart below from center on Budget and Policy Priorities).

As can be also seen from the chart below, businesses get $200+ billion per year in tax breaks or loopholes (no surprise they only contribute less than 20% to the government revenue).

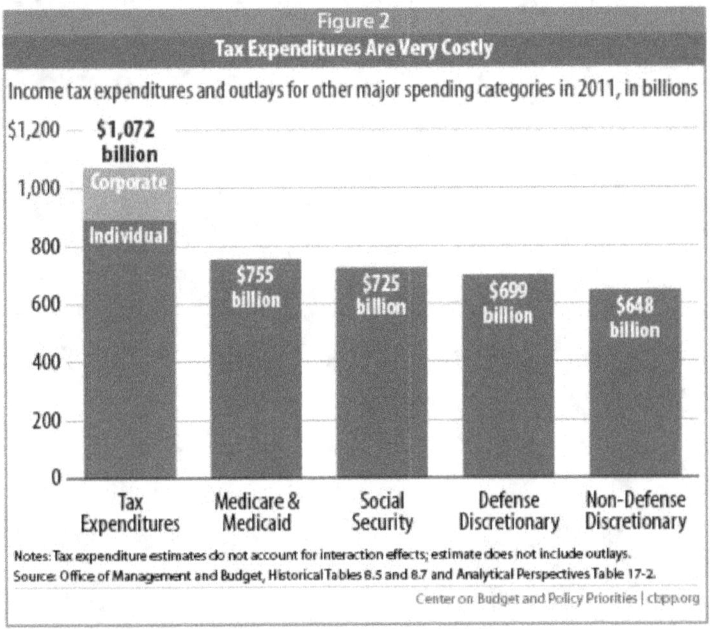

So the bottom line is that both parties spend as we have seen in the previous chapter. In fact, they have increased the national debt almost equally. However, the Democrats increased the debt by increases in social programs, by using direct spending methods, which makes this spending very visible.

Republicans on the other hand, increased the debt by giving larger tax breaks but by accounting for this as tax expenditures which remain under the radar and not very transparent.

And neither party fully balanced the budget resulting in deficits going up through the roof.

So, another myth of Republicans that Democrats are the spending party is debunked,

GDP by State

In this chapter we will look at the statistics based on the GDP contribution by Democratic v/s Republican states. My initial thought was to look at this from state governorship point of view as the state's economy is dependent more upon who is governing it more than who the president is. But honestly this is not an easy statistic to look at since the leadership in some states changes parties from election to election. So, looking at it this way becomes a point-in-time view rather than a trend.

To avoid this, I thought it makes sense to look at the GDP numbers by dividing the states into "solid" Democratic v/s "solid" Republican which tend to stay with one party over a longer period and therefore give us a trend.

| 2012 GDP By State (based solid D or solid R states) | | | | | |
| Democratic States | | Republican States | | Swing States | |
State	Total	State	Total	State	Total
California	1,751,002	Texas	1,211,692	Florida	672,287
New York	1,038,541	Georgia	374,000	Pennsylvania	511,345
Illinois	594,201	Indiana	255,380	Ohio	435,104
New Jersey	438,173	Tennessee	240,523	North Carolina	392,905
Massachusetts	353,717	Arizona	230,641	Virginia	385,772
Michigan	348,867	Missouri	221,702	Minnesota	252,971
Washington	325,165	Louisiana	198,548	Wisconsin	225,094
Maryland	274,930	Alabama	157,272	Iowa	129,799
Colorado	239,884	South Carolina	150,596	West Virginia	56,384
Connecticut	197,202	Kentucky	146,829		
Oregon	187,440	Oklahoma	138,296		
Nevada	113,197	Kansas	118,523		
DC	92,106	Utah	111,808		
New Mexico	70,699	Arkansas	93,892		
Hawaii	61,877	Mississippi	86,396		
New Hampshire	56,735	Nebraska	83,393		
Delaware	56,110	Idaho	50,976		
Maine	45,986	Alaska	44,732		
Rhode Island	43,774	North Dakota	38,654		
Vermont	23,912	South Dakota	35,985		
		Montana	33,374		
		Wyoming	31,302		
Total	6,313,518	Total	4,054,514	Total	3,061,661

As can be seen from the table above, in 2012, the contribution by Democratic states to the nations GDP was $6.3 trillion v/s $4.05 trillion by the Republican states. In fact, if one looks at historical numbers, this trend is consistent through many decades. The Democratic states have constantly contributed more to the nation's economy than the Republican ones. Of course, some of the states that fall into the Democratic column or the Republican column or the Swing column may have changed over the years. One can cherry-pick these states and move them from one column to the other any way they like. But if one divides the states by recent trends, the numbers always favor the Democrats.

If one looks at the data closely, among the Republican states, Texas stands out alone. The GDP of the next state, Georgia, is almost 4 times smaller. Similarly, on the Democratic side the GDP of California and New York stand out. However, Illinois and New Jersey, which are the next states in the table to New York, are not that far behind.

Even if one excludes these outlier states, the GDP from Democratic states still beat the Republican states. For eg: if Texas is excluded, the total GDP from Republican states is $2.8 trillion. On the other hand, if California AND New York are both excluded, the total GDP from Democratic states is $3.5 trillion - significantly more than the GDP from the Republican states.

So, one must ask, how come these Democratic states with their high state taxes and liberal policies towards healthcare and welfare and education are still able to contribute more to the overall GDP? If these liberal states, with their strict regulations and strict environmental policies and high taxes that are so stifling for businesses and the economy, how come the businesses seem to be doing pretty good in their states?

If the conservative policies are indeed better, shouldn't the GDP numbers from the Republican states be higher than the Democrats?

The rhetoric from the Republicans that somehow Democrats are bad for businesses, bad for capitalism, doesn't seem to be holding true out in the real world.

The reason is this; tax policies or regulations alone are not the only thing that matter. It is also the business opportunities that a state provides, the job opportunities a state provide, the business connections a state provides, the infrastructure (airports, ports, highways, power grid etc) the state provides and the ready availability of skilled workers, that also matter (remember, "you didn't build that" tag line from the last election cycle?).

For eg: if you want to open a new software company and are looking for venture capital, I am pretty sure you would not go to Montana or North Dakota. Instead, you may head to California where the venture capitalists are in greater numbers and also where the things you need for your business (software developers, infrastructure etc) are readily available.

Likewise, if you want to get involved in investment banking or finance, you probably head to New York or San Francisco or Chicago rather than to Florida or Nevada, even if the taxes are higher and regulations are stricter in these states.

One might say a lot of states under the Republican column are states with low populations and mostly agricultural economies (eg: Kansas, Minnesota, Indiana, Idaho etc) - which explains the lower GDP. Therefore, it's not fair to compare the GDP of such states to modern economic states under the Democratic column.

Fair point.

But, it is also not fair to say that the Democratic policies are horrible for the economy when in fact they are contributing a lot more to the nation's GDP than their Republican counterparts. The conservative states supposedly have low state taxes and liberal regulatory policies etc. Therefore, one would expect business and people flocking to these states to open up businesses etc.

If one looks at the historical data, the GDP from Democratic states has grown steadily year over year (as did the Republican states). But the Democratic 'liberal' states always contributed more than the Republican states.

Indeed, it is true that over the past couple of years we have seen a net migration of some businesses from liberal states to conservative states – e.g.: from California and New York to Texas and other states. Is this a sign that businesses are indeed moving away from the liberal states? Could be. We must wait and see. My view is that some of this migration is due to the recession and high unemployment situation and higher cost of living in these states. As people are unable to find jobs that pay enough to sustain in higher cost of living states, they are moving to other states because the cost of living is lower. For eg: someone making minimum wage in Austin, TX may be in a better living position than someone making minimum wage in San Francisco simply because of the significant difference in cost of living between these two cities even though the minimum wage in San Francisco is almost double that of minimum wage in Austin.

Taxes, Taxes and Taxes

During the 2012 presidential campaign, Mitt Romney, the Republican candidate for president, was secretly videotaped telling wealthy fundraisers that 47% of Americans do not pay taxes. He went on to say that these Americans are "dependent on the government" and feel "entitled to health care, to food, to housing, to you-name-it."

What he failed to mention is that a vast majority of these bottom 47%, do indeed pay payroll taxes, property taxes, sales taxes, state taxes etc.

In 2012, about 18% of the tax filers did not pay neither federal nor payroll taxes as most of those likely are elderly Americans whose only source of income is Social Security. They don't have to pay federal income taxes on income from Social Security if it is under $25,000 for single filers or under $35,000 if filing jointly. And they are not required to pay payroll taxes, as Social Security payments are not **earned** income. Thus, 18% of the US population did not pay any federal or payroll taxes because they are **NOT REQUIRED** to. This group may still have paid property taxes and state taxes and sales taxes.

The next batch of Americans, about 6%, had **earned** income less than $20,000 and therefore didn't owe any taxes, but they indeed paid payroll taxes and may have paid state taxes, sales taxes and even property taxes.

The rest paid federal taxes.

So, to assert that 47% do not pay any taxes is a bogus assertion. If Mitt Romney meant to say 47% do not pay any *Federal* taxes, even this assertion would have been bogus, since as we have just seen above, only 24% do not pay any Federal taxes (18% + 6%). And most of these 24% don't pay federal taxes because their income is low, and they are not required to pay Federal taxes. As stated above, some may pay payroll taxes, state taxes and sales taxes.

Revisiting the fairness doctrine from the previous chapter, one must ask, why is it that these 24% who did not pay any federal taxes because of the tax code that required them not to pay any taxes becomes a problem when those claiming $1million mortgage deductions and reducing their taxes is not a problem? How come Romney never mentioned these tax deductions in his speech?

Romney also said most of these Americans (47%) are "...dependent on the government" and feel "entitled to health care...". Another bogus claim.

There are two medical care programs – Medicare and Medicaid. As we have seen from previous chapters, Medicare is provided to people who have paid into the program via payroll taxes. Thus, it is not considered an entitlement as people have contributed to it throughout their working lives – it is a social *insurance*.

Medicaid on the other hand is a health insurance program designed to cover pregnant women, individuals with disabilities, families with children and the poor.   Other children who do not qualify under Medicaid are covered under CHIP – Children's Health Insurance Program.   According to the Congressional Budget Office, on average in 2012, Medicaid provided health coverage for 54 million Americans and 5 million children under CHIPS. As the chart below shows, most of the participants are children, followed by Non-Disabled Adults, followed by Disabled, followed by Low Income Seniors and Pregnant Women.

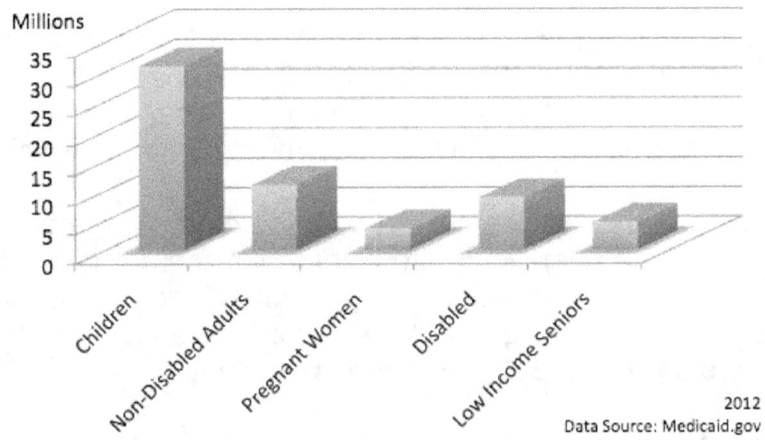

The number of individuals covered under Medicaid was 59 million in 2012 and comes to about 18% of the total US population and not 47% as Romney claims. He probably included Medicare in that number but as we have mentioned before, people getting Medicare benefits pay for it through payroll taxes.

Now, it is true that over the past couple of decades, an increasingly smaller group at the top is paying most of the income taxes. For eg: the following table from www.taxfoundation.com shows that in 2009, almost 90% of the federal income taxes were paid by the top 25% of earners and less than 3% paid by the bottom 50%.

Federal Income Tax Payments by Income Percentile - 2009				
Income Percentile	Income Taxes Paid ($ millions)	Group's Share of Total AGI	Group's Share of Income Taxes	Average Tax Rate
All Taxpayers	$865,863	100.0%	100.0%	11.1%
Top 1%	$318,043	16.9%	36.7%	24.0%
Top 5%	$507,907	31.7%	58.7%	20.5%
Top 10%	$610,156	43.2%	70.5%	18.1%
Top 25%	$755,903	65.8%	87.3%	14.7%
Top 50%	$846,352	86.5%	97.7%	12.5%
Bottom 50%	$19,511	13.5%	2.3%	1.8%

An interesting thing to note is that the top 50% earned $32K and above and the bottom 50% of US tax filers earned 32K or below! So, is it any surprise that the earners in the bottom 50% pay less in taxes and probably rely on some form of government help?

If one looks at the income growth over the past few decades, it is clear most of the wage increase went to the top earners. In fact, according to The Economic Policy Institute, the income for the top 1% increased by 128% whereas for the remaining 99% the income went up by 2.3% over the past 30 years!

Clearly the government policies should do more to increase the income level of the bottom 99% so they could earn more and also contribute in paying taxes.

Lets take a look at another statistic. As you can see from the below table, the vast majority of the 2012 Federal taxes paid are from Democratic states - there is no contest. By a wide margin, the Democratic states paid $1.18 trillion v/s $717 billion from Republican states and $613 billion from Swing states.

Democratic States	Total Federal Rev	Republican States	Total Federal Rev	Swing States	Total Federal Rev
California	292,563,574	Texas	219,459,878	Florida	122,249,635
New York	201,167,954	Georgia	65,498,308	Ohio	111,094,276
Illinois	124,431,227	Indiana	51,238,512	Pennsylvania	108,961,515
New Jersey	111,377,490	Missouri	48,413,247	Minnesota	78,685,402
Massachusetts	79,826,976	Tennessee	47,010,303	Virginia	64,297,400
Michigan	59,210,158	Arizona	34,850,436	North Carolina	61,600,064
Washington	52,443,862	Louisiana	34,811,072	Wisconsin	41,498,033
Maryland	48,107,002	Oklahoma	27,087,264	Iowa	18,753,596
Connecticut	47,262,702	Arkansas	25,299,832	West Virginia	6,498,502
Colorado	41,252,701	Kentucky	25,085,813		
Oregon	22,716,602	Kansas	21,904,615		
Delaware	21,835,412	Alabama	20,882,949		
DC	20,747,652	Nebraska	19,795,254		
Nevada	13,727,425	South Carolina	18,557,166		
Rhode Island	10,992,338	Utah	15,642,129		
New Hampshire	8,807,691	Mississippi	10,458,549		
New Mexico	7,866,206	Idaho	7,622,490		
Hawaii	6,511,578	North Dakota	5,664,860		
Maine	6,229,189	South Dakota	5,136,249		
Vermont	3,524,887	Alaska	4,898,780		
		Montana	4,383,727		

The above table is from www.taxfoundation.org. It shows federal tax revenue from each state for 2012. The total revenue includes business taxes and individual income taxes. I added the categorization of states into

Just like before, it's very possible you may not agree with how the states have been categorized into Democratic and the Republican columns. Please go ahead and reassign them yourself and see what happens - just make sure your assignments are realistic and are not completely skewed one way or the other.

Some of you may be wondering, since federal tax rates are the same no matter which state one lives in, how does individual state policies impact federal taxes? Good question. The point I am trying to make here is this. If the state policies towards regulations, environment, state income taxes, property taxes and local taxes etc are bad, wouldn't the businesses and the people move away from these states to states that have more friendly policies?   And once they move there, they would eventually pay federal taxes from those states.

And there is no doubt some migration between states is occurring year over year. But if one looks at the figures over an extended period of time, the Democratic states consistently contribute more to the federal revenue than their Republican counterparts. The reason is that tax policies or the regulations alone are not the only thing that matter (as mentioned in the previous chapter). It is also the business opportunities, job opportunities, business connections, infrastructure and high skill set of readily available employees, jobs etc that also matter.

Let's now look at how corporate taxes fare against individual income taxes. As the chart below shows, 55% of the federal revenue comes from individual income taxes and 11.2% from corporate income taxes, 31% from payroll taxes and the rest from Estate, Gift and Excise taxes. The data is from irs.gov and is for the year 2012.

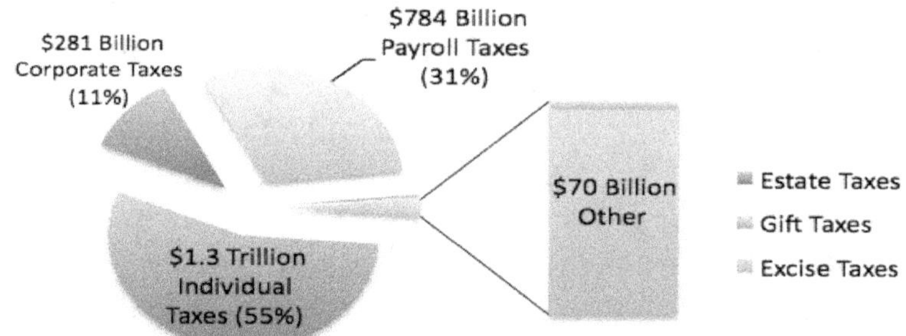

The payroll taxes include FICA (Social Security & Medicare), SECA (Self employed equivalent of FICA), disability insurance, unemployment insurance and railroad retirement taxes. Employers pay the full unemployment taxes, which was about 0.3 of the total taxes. Employees and employers split 50/50 the FICA taxes. SECA is fully paid by the self-employed. The problem is because some of these numbers (SECA, FICA, etc) are grouped together, it is not easy to identify the FICA taxes and therefore the FICA taxes paid by the employers cannot be determined. To keep the calculations simple we will assign 15% of payroll taxes to employees and 16% to employers.

This means, including their portion of the payroll taxes, individuals paid 70% of taxes and employers paid 27% of the taxes. The corporate taxes collected are some of the lowest ever collected while the individual income taxes are among the highest ever collected. The graph below clearly shows the corporate income taxes paid have been going down steadily over the past decades.

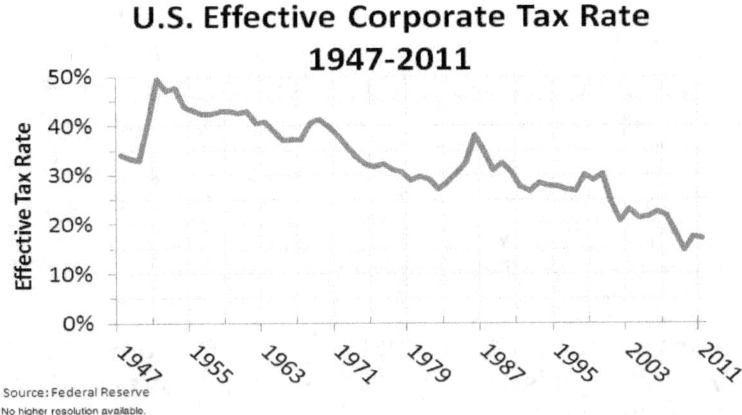

One caveat: normally, LLCs and S Corporations, which are businesses, allow their owners to treat their share of the profits as their personal income and pay taxes at their personal tax rates. Therefore, this "business" profit is shifted into the individual income category. Some people claim that because of this shifting of income, the corporate taxes collected "appear" to be lower than what they actually are. This is somewhat true. But, the revenue from LLCs and S Corporations is so insignificant I don't believe it shifts the ratios significantly.

I am sure you often hear from conservatives that corporate tax rates are at their highest rates in years and that they are at the top of the scale when compared with other western nations. This may be true. The tax rates may be higher, but the problem is corporations don't always pay at the tax rates they are supposed to – most of them actually pay at a lower rate. Their "**effective tax rate**" is much lower due to the tax breaks and loopholes (eg: offshore tax shelters) and other tax incentives provided to them (you might want to read this interesting report from Government Accountability Office on Corporate Profits).

As the chart below shows, corporate **profits** are at their highest since World War II and yet the corporate taxes paid are among the lowest. So, despite the loud noise from the Republicans about high corporate taxes, the numbers don't seem to support that claim. It actually turns out individual taxpayers are contributing more and more to the federal revenue. And even though the corporations' use the general resources and infrastructure paid for by the individual taxpayers, they seem to be paying less and less in tax revenue.

For eg: FedEx relies almost completely on the roads and bridges and airports for its existence and is using the infrastructure paid for mostly by the individuals and reaping huge profits but has only paid less than 5% in federal taxes over the past 5 years. Yes, it did pay state and local taxes etc....but, so did the individual taxpayers. One of the reasons why FedEx paid such low taxes may be related to the accelerated depreciation of assets benefit the government allows. The rationale for this benefit was it supposedly would create more jobs. Nevertheless, this is a "benefit" that was provided to companies and FedEx is taking advantage of it.

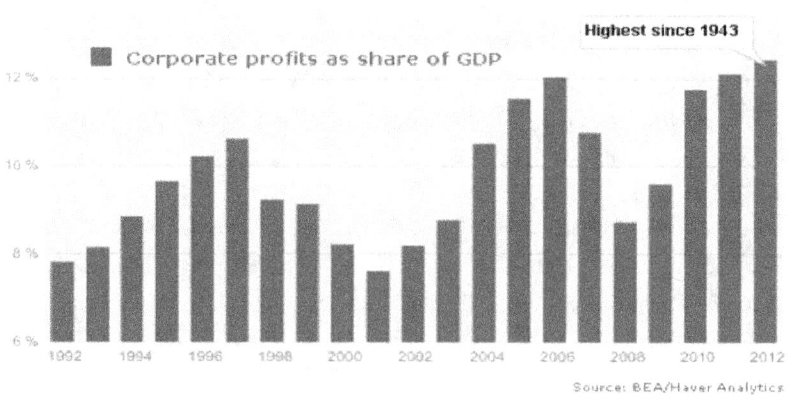

Profits at highest levels since World War II

Next, let's look at how these taxes shifted over the years. As the chart below (data from whitehouse.gov) shows, over the years (from 1934 through 2011) the corporate tax revenue has gone down and payroll tax revenue has gone up. As mentioned above, both the employees and the employers contribute to the payroll taxes. If you noticed, the individual income tax revenue pretty much remained the same over 76 years and took a dip around 2004/2005 (courtesy of George W tax cuts).

But the payroll taxes went up significantly. And half of these taxes are paid by the individuals. Thus, if one adds the individual tax plus half the payroll tax paid by individuals, the individual's contribution to the overall tax revenue went up significantly.

On the other hand, the revenue contribution from corporate income taxes went down significantly from the 1930s. However, the portion of the payroll taxes went up even for corporations as businesses pay part of the payroll taxes. But even taking into account that half of payroll taxes are added to the corporate taxes, the net effect is that corporate tax revenue contribution went down significantly over the years.

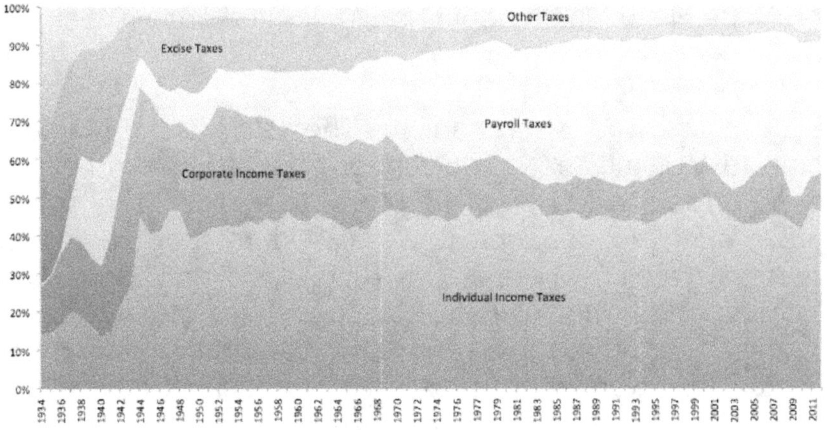

K-12 Education

According to the GOP party platform, the federal government, since 1965 "...has spent $2 trillion on elementary and secondary education with no substantial improvement in academic achievement or high school graduation rates (which currently are 59 percent for African-American students and 63 percent for Hispanics). The U.S. spends an average of more than $10,000 per pupil per year in public schools, for a total of more than $550 billion. That represents more than 4 percent of GDP devoted to K-12 education in 2010. Of that amount, federal spending was more than $47 billion. Clearly, if money were the solution, our schools would be problem-free."

But, a new report (see table next page) from the Department of Education official blog dated January 23, 2013 shows that high school graduation rates are at their highest level since 1974. According to a report quoted on this blog, "...this report, during the 2009-10 school year, 78.2 percent of high school students nationwide graduated on time, which is a substantial increase from the 73.4 percent recorded in 2005-6. The report shows that graduation rates were up for all ethnic groups in 2010, and that the rate for Hispanic students has jumped almost 10 points since 2006".

Clearly, there is a discrepancy. The GOP platform statement seems to indicate that even though the government has spent over $2 trillion in the past 48 years, there is "... no substantial improvement in academic achievement or high school graduation rates", whereas the report from the Department of Education seems to indicate that there was indeed substantial progress. As the table from the Department of Education indicates, the graduation rates from high school have increased across board except in a few states like Nevada, Connecticut, Utah, Arkansas etc, which seem to have major problems.

In the early part of the 1980s, before concerns about the nation's graduation rate and education policies reached front and center on the policy agenda, the high school graduation rates were in the 60-70% range. In the year 2010, the graduation rates were between 70-90%. So, clearly the graduation rates are on the rise despite what Republicans say.

State	HS Grad Rate	Rank	State	HS Grad Rate	Rank
Wyoming	91.90%	1	Delaware	87.40%	27
Minnesota	91.60%	2	District of Colu	87.10%	28
Alaska	91.40%	3	Missouri	86.80%	29
Montana	91.40%	3	Illinois	86.60%	30
New Hampshire	91.20%	5	Indiana	86.60%	30
Vermont	91.00%	6	Virginia	86.60%	30
Utah	90.60%	7	Oklahoma	85.90%	33
Iowa	90.30%	8	Florida	85.50%	34
Nebraska	90.30%	8	Arizona	85.20%	35
Maine	90.20%	10	New York	84.60%	36
Hawaii	90.10%	11	Rhode Island	84.30%	37
North Dakota	90.00%	12	Nevada	84.20%	38
South Dakota	89.80%	13	North Carolina	84.10%	39
Washington	89.80%	13	Georgia	84.00%	40
Wisconsin	89.80%	13	South Carolina	83.60%	41
Colorado	89.70%	16	Tennessee	83.20%	42
Kansas	89.50%	17	New Mexico	83.10%	43
Massachusetts	88.90%	18	Arkansas	82.70%	44
Oregon	88.90%	18	West Virginia	82.60%	45
Connecticut	88.60%	20	Alabama	81.90%	46
Idaho	88.50%	21	Kentucky	81.70%	47
Michigan	88.40%	22	Louisiana	81.60%	48
Maryland	88.20%	23	California	80.80%	49
Pennsylvania	87.90%	24	Texas	80.40%	50
Ohio	87.80%	25	Mississippi	80.30%	51
New Jersey	87.60%	26			

The vast majority of the cost of K12 education (over 90%) is borne by the state and local government. This is paid for either via property taxes, local taxes or other means. The federal government pays about $47 billion to $76 billion per year depending on who is reporting the figures and what is included in that number. For example, some include the cost of federal tax credits while others only include the federal grants to states.

The limited funding provided by the federal government comes with strings attached. For eg: even though Congress has increased funding for the schools over the years, it has at the same time imposed layers of rules and regulations on local school districts. For eg: the No Child Left Behind Act (George W's signature education reform) that was passed in 2002 imposed rules for state academic standards, student testing, and related regulations. These regulations resulted in a backlash from the state governments because they created additional bureaucracies of school administrators while at the same time inadvertently suppressed innovation and diversity in state education systems.

In any case, there is no question; the cost of K2 education is primarily a responsibility of the state and local governments. And, for the most part the education policies are set at the state and local level.

So, let's see how the states have fared in funding education and the results. The table below lists the increase in funding by each state since 2002 in addition to listing the percent increase or decrease in graduation rates.

State	+/- % Graduation	Increase in funding	Party	State	+/- % Graduation	Increase in funding	Party
Nevada	-14.5%	39%	R	Washington	3.0%	35%	D
Connecticut	-5.8%	37%	D	Colorado	3.4%	36%	D
Utah	-1.6%	39%	R	Texas	3.4%	43%	R
Arkansas	-1.6%	46%	R	Minnesota	3.4%	29%	S
Nebraska	-1.4%	38%	R	Florida	4.1%	37%	S
Rhode Island	-1.3%	32%	D	California	4.1%	31%	D
Arizona	-1.2%	37%	R	Hawaii	4.1%	35%	D
South Dakota	-1.2%	38%	R	New Mexico	4.2%	43%	D
New Jersey	0.2%	35%	D	Louisiana	4.7%	38%	R
DC	0.3%	54%	D	Wisconsin	5.3%	30%	S
Virginia	0.6%	37%	S	Missouri	5.4%	29%	R
Montana	0.9%	35%	R	Illinois	6.0%	31%	D
Mississippi	1.1%	32%	R	Wyoming	6.4%	52%	R
Indiana	1.7%	27%	R	Maine	6.5%	31%	D
Michigan	1.9%	19%	D	North Carolina	6.8%	37%	S
North Dakota	2.0%	41%	R	Massachusetts	6.9%	33%	D
Pennsylvania	2.4%	32%	S	Alabama	7.1%	40%	R
Ohio	2.4%	33%	S	Alaska	7.5%	41%	R
Delaware	2.5%	44%	D	Kansas	7.6%	36%	R
Oklahoma	2.5%	33%	R	Vermont	7.8%	42%	D
Oregon	2.6%	35%	D	New Hampshire	8.1%	39%	D
Idaho	2.6%	28%	R	Kentucky	8.2%	42%	R
West Virginia	2.6%	41%	S	South Carolina	8.5%	36%	R
Iowa	2.6%	36%	S	Georgia	9.1%	34%	R
Maryland	3.0%	39%	D	New York	15.1%	38%	D
Washington	3.0%	35%	D	Tennessee	17.0%	31%	R

As can be seen, Nevada has the highest increase in funding (39%) and yet its graduation rates are negative 14.5%. Likewise, Connecticut is next with a negative 5.8% graduation rate even with a 37% increase in funding.

If one takes a look at the top 20 *under* performers, from Nevada to Oklahoma, 11 of these states are solid Republican, 6 are solid Democratic and 3 are swing states.

Since K12 education is mostly state and local funding and the educational policies are mostly controlled at the state and local levels, one wonders why 11 of the top worst performing states just happen to be Republican? I mean, if Republicans have better educational policies and have a better way to spend the educational funding, shouldn't these states be the best performers?

Now, there is some good news for the Republicans. The state of

Tennessee achieved a 17% increase in graduation rates - the highest in the nation. So, clearly Tennessee must be doing something right.

I am sure you have heard a lot of noise from the Republicans about how our education system is broken despite the skyrocketing spending on education. There is no argument the education system is broken - it needs to be revamped with a focus on science and math and getting parents involved in the decision making process and getting the most for our money.

These are all critical goals and must be pursued. But, if one listens to the Republican drumbeat, one may get the impression that all these problems are related to the Democrats policies and Republicans have nothing to do with it. Even though the Republicans seem to imply they have better solutions, the actual results indicate otherwise.

I am sure there are many Democratic policies that are bad; but there must be Republican policies that are bad too. The fact that 11 out of 20 worst performing states are solid Republican states demonstrate that.

Look, this is a broken system all around. It's not just a Democratic problem nor is it just a Republican problem. This is a common American problem. Maybe the politicians should approach it as a common problem and try to work with each other in finding common solutions. This constant rhetoric from both parties is poisoning the minds and dividing us and preventing us from finding common practical solutions.

I honestly believe education is a bigger problem for the next generation than deficits and debt. Why? Because, if our kids are not well educated to compete in the global economy for jobs, it does not matter even if the deficit is down to zero. We will still have high unemployment rates and much lower standard of living and the overall GDP will shrink. On the other hand, if we have a well-educated generation that can compete for the highest paying jobs, we can always pay down the debt, since the revenues will continue to flow.

Another reason is, as the baby-boomers start retiring in large numbers over the next decade or so, the younger generation has to shift into the jobs vacated by the retiring boomers. If they are not educated, they will be unable to fill these jobs, which will either get shifted overseas or filled by someone hired from overseas.

Therefore, laying a solid foundation in K12 is no doubt very important. It sets the stage for the next stage in a kid's life - higher education. Which is what we will look at next.

The State of Higher Education

Why the focus on higher education? Because, quite simply, higher education is where the opportunities and America's future will depend on (if not already). We tend to focus a lot on K12 and not enough on higher education. We tend to focus on achieving 100% graduation levels from high school but not enough about college attainment levels. In the future, it does not matter if we achieve 100% graduation rate from high school *if the students already graduating are not completing college!* Simply having a high school diploma is not enough!

Therefore, in addition to focusing on achieving higher graduation rates from high schools, we should also focus on getting the 70% or 80% of students *already* graduating from high schools into higher education. Why is this important? Hopefully, the following chart from the Bureau of Labor Statistics (data from 2012) will tell the story.

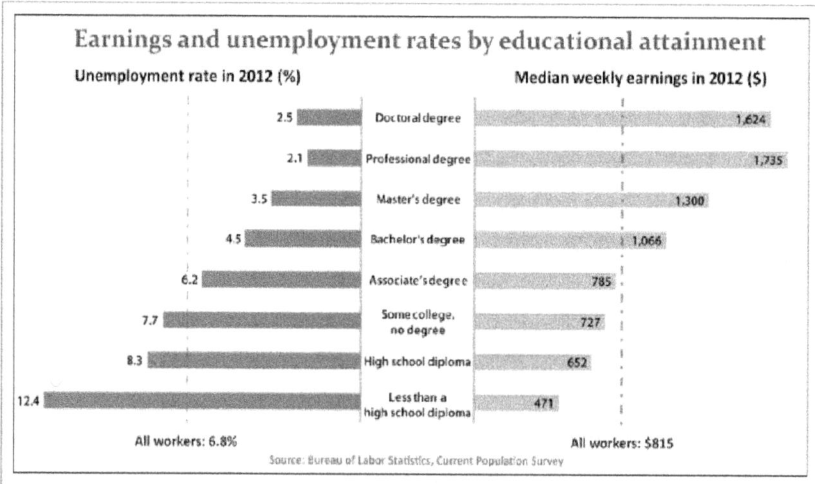

As can be seen (and intuitively know), the lower the education level one has, the less money one makes (I know there are exceptions – we are speaking in general terms here). And they are also more susceptible to unemployment. What is striking is that, even in 2012, when the overall unemployment was high, the unemployment rate for those with bachelor's degrees was under 4.5%. For those with a master's degree it was 3.5%. And the unemployment was even lower for those with professional and doctoral degrees. But, for those with high school diplomas, the unemployment rate was at 8.3% and for those without a high school diploma, a whopping 12.4%!

Likewise, the earning potential also tells a clear story - the higher the education, the higher the potential with those with masters or professional degree earning the most.

But the story goes beyond that. As the chart below from collegeboard.org shows, higher education not only results in higher earning potential, but higher earners also pay higher taxes as well. As people earn more, they pay more in taxes. Therefore, they end up contributing more to society.

Median Earnings and Tax Payments of Full-Time Year-Round Workers Ages 25 and Older, by Education Level, 2008

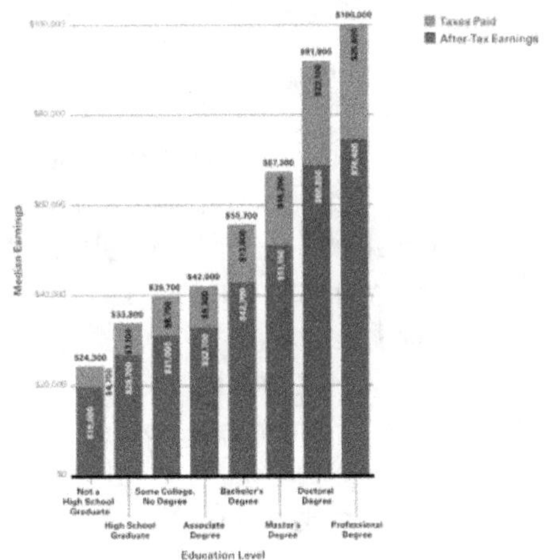

And if you consider earnings over a lifetime, higher earners not only contribute more in taxes, but they contribute more to the economy as they spend more. In addition, they are also less likely to depend on government assistant programs - not only during their earning period, but also after retirement since it is highly likely they may have saved enough to carry them through retirement.

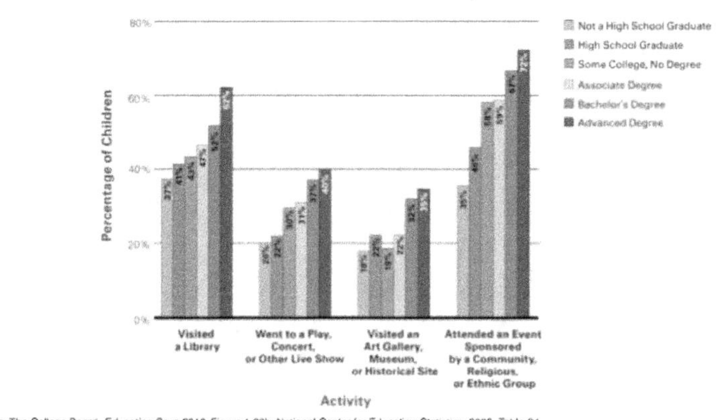

Percentage of Kindergartners Through Fifth-Graders
Whose Parents Reported Participating in Education-Related Activities
with Their Children in the Past Month,
by Parents' Highest Education Level, 2007

Sources: The College Board. *Education Pays 2010*, Figure 1.20b; National Center for Education Statistics, 2009, Table 24.

And, there are other non-monetary benefits as well. For e.g.: the participation rates of those with higher education are very high in their child's education (chart below from collegeboard.org). Studies have shown that higher participation rates by parents in turn results in a higher probability of their kids completing higher education. Which in turn leads to higher probability of *their* children completing higher education. This cycle may continue generation after generation. So, the initial investment in higher education pays off huge dividends in the future over many generations.

Higher education is even more important, considering that in the future manufacturing jobs may become even scarce in the US. Perhaps, several years ago, having a high school diploma was sufficient because there was a direct path to manufacturing jobs that used to pay reasonably well. Unfortunately, this option is no longer available for most Americans with just a high school diploma since most of the manufacturing jobs have either migrated or have been automated. And this trend will continue in the future.

The good news is that Americans have made strides in higher education levels. As the following chart shows, educational attainment from 1940 thru 2009 of individuals in age group 25 and 34 went up significantly.

Education Level of Individuals Ages 25 to 34, 1940–2009

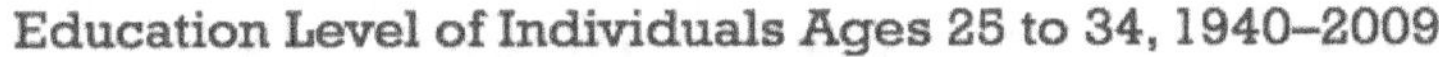
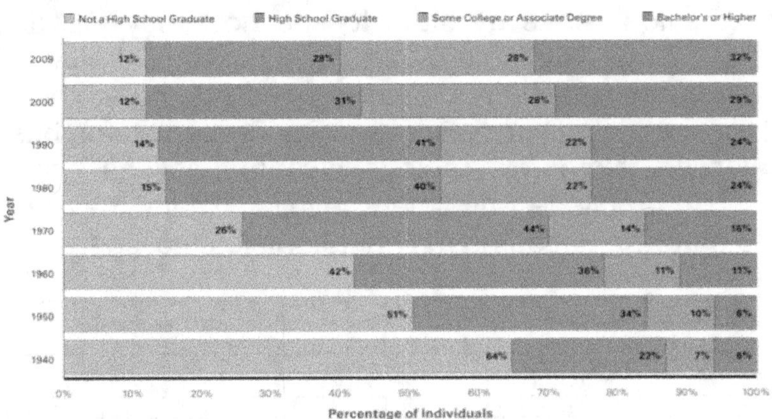

Sources: The College Board, *Education Pays 2010*, Figure 2.7; U.S. Census Bureau, 2009b, Table A-1.

The bad news is, in 2011 the graduation rates for those in the age groups 25-year to 64-years was only 37.8% for 2-year and 4-year college degrees. And over 65% of those in the 25 to 35 year age group still did not even have a bachelor's degree. Yes, some had associate degrees or "some college", but in today's economy, and soon, this is not going to be enough. Today, a bachelor's degree is a must to get a decent job. Ten years from now, even bachelors' degree may not be enough to get good paying jobs in the global economy.   We must lay the groundwork now to attain higher education rates.

On a side note, even though I am focusing on bachelor's degrees and above, even technical diplomas are a lot better than just having a high school diploma.   Therefore, a technical diploma could be a great path for those not wanting to seek bachelor's degrees and above.

As we have seen from the charts above, the decision to pursue higher education should be a no-brainer. But this message is not sinking in. Some states are doing better while others are not so good.

Let's take a look state by state to see how they are doing in achieving college attainment rates.   The table below shows higher education attainment rates as of 2010 by states, which are categorized into Democratic and Republican states based on 2012 election. Note this table shows the college graduation levels and not college enrollment levels.   There may be more students enrolling but some may not complete college.

Democratic Statse	2010 Attainment %	Democratic Statse	2010 Attainment %	Republican States	2010 Attainment %	Republican States	2010 Attainment %
Nevada	28.40%	Pennsylvania	43.90%	Arkansas	28.60%	South Carolina	35.20%
New Mexico	28.70%	Vermont	44.50%	West Virginia	29.50%	Georgia	35.50%
Florida	36.20%	Virginia	44.60%	Louisiana	30.30%	Indiana	36.10%
Delaware	37.20%	Illinois	45.30%	Oklahoma	30.80%	North Carolina	37.60%
Maine	37.20%	Iowa	45.50%	Alabama	31.50%	Utah	38.50%
Michigan	37.20%	Maryland	45.50%	Mississippi	32.10%	Missouri	39.30%
Oregon	37.60%	Connecticut	45.90%	Texas	32.20%	Montana	40.30%
California	37.90%	New Hampshire	46.00%	Idaho	32.70%	South Dakota	42.20%
Ohio	38.00%	New Jersey	47.20%	Tennessee	32.80%	Kansas	42.30%
Hawaii	40.50%	New York	49.60%	Alaska	32.90%	Nebraska	44.20%
Washington	40.90%	Minnesota	49.80%	Arizona	33.00%	North Dakota	50.80%
Wisconsin	41.30%	Massachusetts	54.30%	Kentucky	33.30%		
Rhode Island	42.50%	D.C.	68.80%	Wyoming	34.20%		
Colorado	43.30%						

As can be seen, quite a few states are doing well and many not so. If you believe in the rhetoric from the Republicans, you must think all the states with lower attainment levels must be Democratic, right? Wrong again!

The figures show only 5 Republican states have 40% or more higher education attainment rates. However, there are 18 Democratic states with 40% or higher attainment rates. In fact, under the Democratic column, there are only 9 states with below 40% attainment rates. Contrast this with the Republican states, where 20 states are below 40% attainment rates. There is no doubt Democratic states have significantly better graduation rates. Somehow the Democratic states are managing to do pretty well even with their lousy education policies then their Republican counterparts.

I am not suggesting the numbers from Democratic states are good nor am I suggesting their education policies are great. I completely agree they need revamping. What I am pointing out is, when one looks at the actual results, the Democratic states are doing much better than the Republican states. So, obviously, once again, the Republican rhetoric does not match the numbers.

Let us now look at how higher education is funded in the United States. According to the Institute of Educational Science, as of 2010, the United States had a total of 4,495 Title IV eligible, degree-granting institutions: 2,774 4-year institutions and 1,721 2-year institutions.

It appears that the Federal government funds about $39 billion for higher education. Reason why I say "appears" is that it is hard to figure out the exact number. Jason Delisle in a blog at NYTimes.com alludes to this problem by saying "...most tallies, even official government figures, are incomplete or inaccurate because of the way they treat student loans, refundable tax credits and education programs run by agencies other than the United States Department of Education. Other tallies go too far, lumping veterans' education benefits and other programs into the mix."

Nearly all of the federal higher education spending goes towards students from lower income families. There are four basic programs that account for most of all federal higher education funding. Two of these are grants aids – the Pell Grant program and the Supplemental Education Opportunity Grant Program. In 1996, two new programs were established to aid students from lower income families who meet academic achievements criteria or course of study criteria – Academic Competitiveness Grants and the SMART grants. None of this grant aid has to be paid back and generally may be used to pay for tuition, housing and other expenses at any institution of higher education that the recipient wishes to attend.

The federal government also provides a number of different tax reductions, such as tax credits, tax deductions and tax exemptions to assist individuals and families in paying for a higher education. Generally, federal tax benefits are targeted to middle and upper income individuals and families.

Finally, the Federal government subsidizes student loans to pay for tuition, housing and other costs associated with obtaining a higher education. For the 2012-13 school year, $106.4 billion in new federal student loans were made to students. The students repay most of these loans over the course of their working career so the actual cost to the federal government is significantly less.

It is important to note that the entire federal government spend on education (K12 and higher education) is less than 4% of the overall government budget.

Like the K-12 funding, a majority of the cost of higher education is borne by the state and local governments. As mentioned above, the federal contribution is less than 4% of GDP. Some of the federal money for education flows to the states and the states have a lot of leeway in how they spend it. Therefore, it is mostly the states and local governments deciding on policies and how to spend the federal dollars under broad federal guidelines.

And yet, calls to shut down the Department of Education and to eliminate federal spending abound. The reason? Some claim our education system is so broken and too much money is spent on it without any actual improvement. This despite the evidence that college attainment levels have indeed improved over the years (refer to chart above) and even though a vast majority of education funding comes from states.

Yes, the system is broken and yes, we should be doing better and yes we have a long way to go, but the calls to completely eliminate the Department of Education (instead of fixing it) is pure stupidity. Especially since most of the education policies are set at local levels, we need some national standards that only can be set at the federal level.

Anyway, since the majority of education funding is indeed funded by the states, let's look at how the states are doing in funding higher education. As the table below shows, most of the states have significantly reduced funding for education over the years.

State by State - Higher Education funding Variance from 2007 to 2012

State	% Diff from 2007 to 2012	State	% Diff from 2007 to 2012	State	% Diff from 2007 to 2012
New Hampshire	-33%	Massachusetts	-8%	Connecticut	2%
Arizona	-32%	Minnesota	-8%	New York	2%
South Carolina	-24%	Iowa	-8%	Vermont	3%
Nevada	-20%	Oregon	-7%	Maine	6%
Michigan	-19%	Tennessee	-6%	Indiana	6%
New Mexico	-18%	Kansas	-6%	Nebraska	7%
Florida	-17%	Colorado	-6%	Mississippi	8%
Washington	-16%	Georgia	-5%	Maryland	10%
Pennsylvania	-15%	Missouri	-5%	Texas	13%
Alabama	-13%	Kentucky	-1%	North Carolina	13%
California	-12%	Rhode Island	-1%	Arkansas	13%
Virginia	-12%	Wisconsin	-1%	West Virginia	18%
Louisiana	-12%	South Dakota	0%	Montana	18%
Idaho	-11%	New Jersey	1%	Wyoming	21%
Ohio	-9%	Utah	1%	Alaska	24%
Delaware	-9%	Hawaii	2%	Illinois	26%
Oklahoma	-9%			North Dakota	59%

There are quite a few Republican states and Democrats states at the top of the list with most reductions. States like Arizona, Louisiana, Alabama, Tennessee, Oklahoma and Kentucky all show above 10% reduction in education budgets. On the Democratic side, states like New Hampshire, California, and Washington, Michigan, Oregon etc all show above 10% reduction in education budgets.

This significant reduction in state funding is a recent phenomenon; states have been cutting back on funding because of the budget shortfalls many states are facing due to the recession that started in 2007/2008. It is unfortunate these states have decided to cut education funding rather than find the money elsewhere. Obviously, some politicians don't seem to grasp the importance of education – they say they do, but their actions say something else.

Another interesting statistic comes to light when one compares the state spend on education to the college graduation levels. As the table on the next page shows, some of the states that spend the most on education still fail to deliver higher graduation levels. For eg: West Virginia (a Republican state) spends 8.5%

of its GDP on education and yet has only 17.6% college graduation rates (bachelor's degree). Likewise, Nevada (a Democratic state) spends 4.3% of GDP on education and only delivers 22.2% of college graduates.

So, this spending a lot on education and not delivering is not just a Democratic problem. It is also a Republican problem. And yet, most of the Republicans point to the Democrats for the education system problem. They never seem to acknowledge that the problems are actually worse in Republican controlled states.

One might argue that since most of the Republican states in the south have significant minority populations (African Americans, Hispanics etc), and since the education rates in these populations are usually low (just stating the facts!), this skews the overall stats for these states. In states like Texas, Mississippi, Louisiana, Georgia and Alabama, which have a large population of minorities, the averages may be skewed. But, how does one explain Idaho, Missouri and South Dakota where minority populations are very low and yet these Republican states have low college graduation levels?

State	% With Bachelor Degree	GDP %	Party	State	% With Bachelor Degree	GDP %	Party
W Virginia	17.6%	8.5%	R	Maine	27.1%	6.5%	D
Arkansas	19.6%	7.9%	R	Alaska	27.2%	6.8%	R
Mississippi	19.7%	6.9%	R	Georgia	27.5%	5.8%	R
Kentucky	20.6%	6.7%	R	Nebraska	27.8%	5.8%	R
Louisiana	21.1%	5.1%	R	Delaware	28.0%	5.0%	D
Alabama	22.0%	7.4%	R	Montana	28.2%	6.7%	R
Nevada	22.2%	4.3%	D	Oregon	29.0%	5.4%	D
Indiana	22.7%	5.7%	R	Hawaii	29.5%	5.0%	D
Oklahoma	23.0%	5.4%	R	Utah	29.6%	6.4%	R
Tennessee	23.0%	4.7%	R	Kansas	29.7%	6.0%	R
South Carolina	24.2%	6.9%	R	California	30.2%	5.2%	D
Wyoming	24.2%	6.5%	R	Rhode Island	30.6%	6.0%	D
Ohio	24.5%	6.7%	D	Illinois	30.7%	5.1%	D
Idaho	24.6%	5.2%	R	Washington	31.4%	5.3%	D
Iowa	24.9%	6.6%	D	Minnesota	31.8%	5.4%	D
Michigan	25.3%	7.2%	D	New York	32.5%	6.0%	D
Missouri	25.4%	5.2%	R	New Hampshire	33.1%	6.1%	D
New Mexico	25.4%	8.5%	D	Vermont	33.8%	8.9%	D
South Dakota	25.8%	5.1%	R	Virginia	34.4%	5.2%	D
Florida	26.0%	5.1%	D	New Jersey	35.0%	5.9%	D
Wisconsin	26.0%	6.8%	D	Connecticut	35.7%	5.4%	D
Texas	26.1%	5.3%	R	Maryland	36.1%	5.8%	D
Arizona	26.4%	5.0%	R	Colorado	36.3%	4.9%	D
North Carolina	26.5%	5.3%	R	Massachusetts	38.7%	4.9%	D
North Dakota	26.5%	5.3%	R	DC	50.5%	2.1%	D
Pennsylvania	26.7%	6.0%	D				

Let's also look at a few other stats. Take a look at the following few charts which are from www.college.completion.com which is a micro-site of The Chronicle of Higher Education and is supported by Bill & Melinda Gates Foundation. The first chart shows public colleges by state. As can be seen, a vast majority of the public colleges are located in the northeast, mid-west or west coast (mostly democratic states) with a few in the south - mostly in the Carolinas and Florida and Texas.

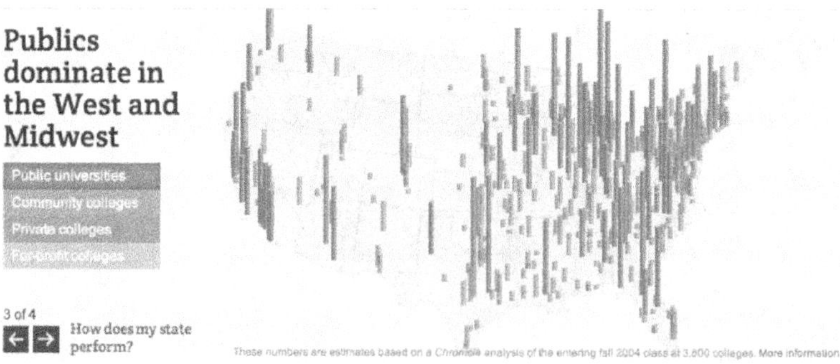

The next couple of charts show the community colleges across the US and the private colleges across the US, most of which are distributed in the northeast or California and Illinois or Michigan with some here and there.

Obviously, these colleges are located where most of the population is. That is why you see vast areas in the middle of the map where there are not many colleges. And also some of this is historical, as some of the private institutions, especially in the northeast, were established a long time ago.

And of course, as far as the public institutions (universities and community colleges) are concerned, state funding is critical to their continued success. This might explain why the Republicans want to cut education funding; since there aren't that many colleges in their states anyway, they probably don't care.

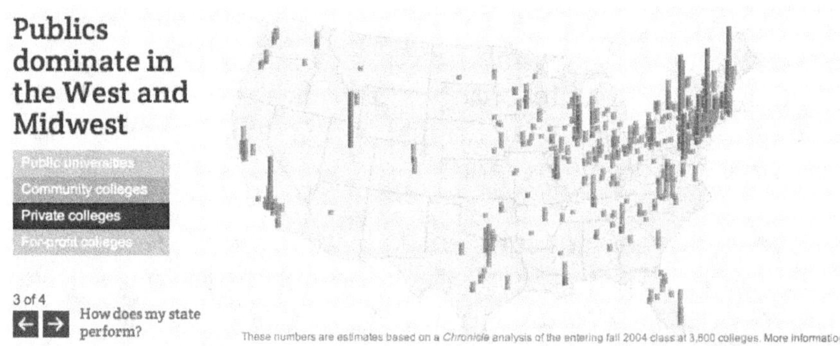

Rep. Ron Paul (R-Texas), is quoted as saying "You have a right to your life and you have a right to your property, but you don't have, education isn't a right, healthcare isn't, education…these are things you have to earn."

This, in my opinion, is a very myopic view.

The whole society benefits when more people get college education. The argument on the other side is, why should my tax dollars pay for your kids' education, especially, when your kid will be the main beneficiary? This is a silly argument on many fronts.

First of all, people with a college education earn more and therefore contribute more in taxes where everybody benefits.

Secondly, people with college education go into research and develop new medicines, new cures for deadly diseases, innovate and make things better for everyone. At a macro level, this benefits the whole society and increases the overall GDP.

Thirdly, let's say we keep reducing funding for education – eventually, there will be less and less college-educated population. And guess what happens next? Most of the jobs that require college education either will have to hire from overseas or move the jobs overseas. This not only puts

America's competitive edge at risk, but also puts at risk the high standards of living and puts at risk its entire economy. In fact, some of this is already occurring.

Case in point, look at the following excerpt from a story in Seattletimes.com dated March 28, 2013.

> "It's never been easy — and it may be getting harder — to find an unemployed computer-science major in Washington state.
>
> "Just ask Steve Singh, the CEO of a company with 700 job openings worldwide — 300 of them in Washington."
>
> "We have a standing discussion with University of Washington computer science — anybody you graduate, we'll take," said Singh, CEO of Redmond-based Concur Technologies.
>
> "This week, the business group Washington Roundtable released a study that says 25,000 high-skill jobs in Washington are going unfilled — jobs that have remained vacant for three months or longer, because qualified workers can't be found to fill them."

Fourthly, because college educated people earn more, they are less likely to become a burden on the "welfare" system. Even though this great recession hit a lot of people including those with professional and college degrees, imagine how quickly we would have got out of this, if we had 80-90% college graduation levels instead of the 40% we are at now? There would have been a lot less people at the 12.5% unemployment levels.

And, lastly, lack of college education also leads to deterioration of the middle class. Because good paying jobs will not be available for those with high school diplomas or lower, they end up working for lower wages. This sets up a race to the bottom.

So, Rep Ron Paul's assertion that education is not a right but must be earned may sound logical at face value, but when one looks at it from a macro level, the government (and thus the society) and the individual are both benefiting from this individual getting a higher education. Therefore, both have a stake in it.

American graduation rates in the STEM (Science, Technology, Engineering and Math) fields are abysmal. As the following <u>chart</u> shows, only 4% of high school graduates eventually graduate in STEM.

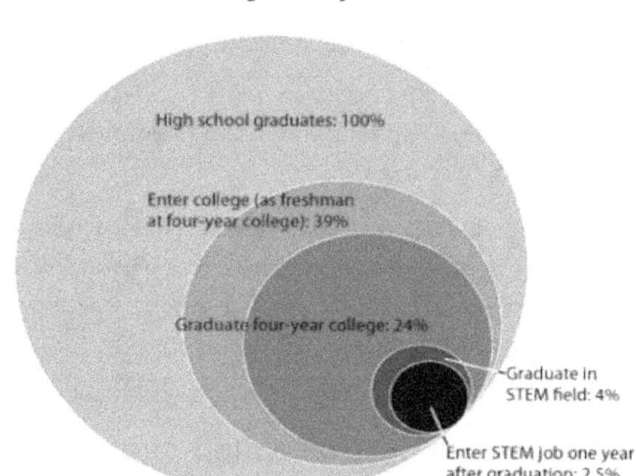

Source: Authors' analysis of National Center for Education Statistics (2009b, 2013)

There is no doubt that in the future global economy, we need to compete with China and India where 40% or more of their graduates come out with degrees in STEM. And keep in mind, the populations of China and India combined (2.4Billion) is about 7 times greater than the US. So, just in pure numbers there are millions more STEM graduates coming out of just these two countries. Therefore, there is no question why there should be urgency for the U.S. to develop a stronger workforce in STEM fields.

In the book, The World is Flat, released in 2005, Thomas

Friedman, describes how various events including the internet revolution made it possible for people around the globe to participate in a global economy. These people from all over the globe already had the brains - all they needed was a way to connect into the global economy. The Internet provided that capability. Friedman argued that for the US to compete in this new economy, our workforce has to become more adaptable.

Even now I clearly remember one thing that he said in the book, which I recall I made sure my kids understood. He said "...every young American would be wise to think of himself or herself as competing against every young Chinese, Indian or Brazilian. In Globalization 1.0, *countries* [emphasis added] had to think globally to thrive, or at least survive. In Globalization 2.0, *companies* [not countries] had to think globally to thrive, or at least survive. In Globalization 3.0, *individuals* [emphasis added] have to think globally to thrive, or at least survive."

That's right, in the future (if not already) you as an individual will be competing globally for your job. You are not competing locally in your city or your state or the country – you are competing globally for your job. And remember all those STEM graduates from China and India? You will be competing with millions of them for your job.

Well, we are already at Globalization 3.0 and Friedman was right. The problem is most of the people did not heed this warning. And the government did nothing in terms of changing policies and diverting funds to help people get technical education or higher education and training in areas where their skills become adaptable. And we are paying the price now and will continue to do so until something is done.

Takers v/s Makers

During the 2012 election, Republicans made a lot of noise about takers v/s makers. They described a narrative which implied that on one hand are people who work hard, are responsible, are self-reliant and pay taxes and keep the economy going and on the other are those who mooch off the government. And of course, who can forget the infamous 47% from Mitt Romney?

As we have noted in the Taxes, Taxes and Taxes chapter, even though the 47% may not pay federal income tax, most do pay payroll taxes, they pay property taxes and they pay state and local taxes. And many of them are senior citizens living on social security, which they paid into and are now simply collecting what's due to them. As the chart below shows, only about 6.9% of the tax filers actually do not pay any federal taxes because they make $20,000 or under. Of the remaining, 28.3% pay payroll taxes (and maybe even state and local taxes) and 10.3% are elderly living on social security etc.

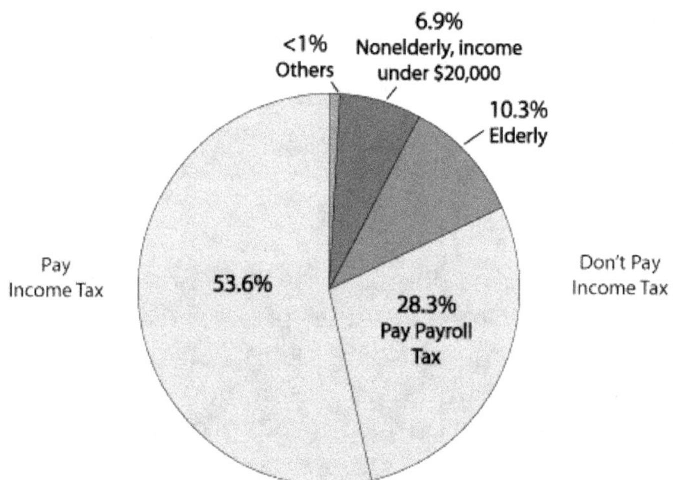

And part of the reason why so many Americans do not pay any federal taxes is because the Republicans have passed a series of tax cuts that not only benefited the higher income earner, but also eliminated the taxes for the lower income earners. They had to do this so the Democrats could go along with the tax cuts on the high-income earners. So, this was a throw-in. Reagan and George W's tax cuts created this mess, which, by the way, was not paid for. So, of course the national debt went up.

But here's a funny thing. The conservatives have now become so incensed that the national debt is out of control (even though they were responsible for half of it), that they are now proposing more tax cuts for the higher income earners and paying for it by cutting the social benefits for the poor.

And by the way, as we have seen in chapter 3, the national debt went up over $4 trillion under George W Bush because of the unpaid wars and tax cuts. As a matter of fact he reversed the budget surpluses that Clinton left him. So, here's a question. Where was the tea party then? Were they a slumber party for 8 years of George W and woke up all of a sudden in 2009 when Obama became president and realized the debt was out of control? How come we have not seen a single tea partier holding a rally about debt during George W?

Are we to believe they had no clue that the debt was going up under George W? Or, maybe the reason why they had not made any noise is because George W was a Republican and it was OK to raise the debt because, hey, after all they were getting tax cuts. So, why complain?

In 2009 when Obama became president, they knew tax cuts would be eliminated, so of course, *now* they have problems with the debt.

On a side note about "taker" v/s "makers", it is interesting to note that some of the same people who complain about national debt, who complain about the social programs, who complain about the food stamps etc, are actually benefitting from these same programs! Here's an excerpt from an article in Nytimes.com dated February 11, 2011 that highlights this hypocrisy.

"Ki Gulbranson owns a logo apparel shop, deals in jewelry on the side and referees youth soccer games. He makes about $39,000 a year and wants you to know that he does not need any help from the federal government.

"I don't demand that the government does this for me. I don't feel like I need the government," said KI GULBRANSON, who counts on an earned-income tax credit and has signed up his children for free meals at school.

He says that too many Americans lean on taxpayers rather than living within their means. He supports politicians who promise to cut government spending. In 2010, he printed T-shirts for the Tea Party campaign of a neighbor, Chip Cravaack, who ousted this region's long-serving Democratic congressman.

Yet this year, as in each of the past three years, Mr. Gulbranson, 57, is counting on a payment of several thousand dollars from the federal government, a subsidy for working families called the earned-income tax credit. He has signed up his three school-age children to eat free breakfast and lunch at federal expense. And Medicare paid for his mother, 88, to have hip surgery twice."

Some of the conservatives have become so blinded by the rhetoric or have gotten so completely brainwashed, that they don't even recognize their own hypocrisy. They complain about others and yet they do the same thing.

Recently you may have heard in the news about a spat between New Jersey Governor, Chris Christie and Rep. Rand Paul. This issue started with the New Jersey Governor asking for federal disaster relief for hurricane Sandy victims. Mr. Paul accused the New Jersey Governor of, "…bankrupting the government and not allowing enough money to be left over for national defense…" by being a "…Gimme, gimme, gimme all my Sandy money now…" state.

Chris Christie responded by accusing Rand Paul of being, "…the king of bacon talking about bacon," He went on to say, "…I find it interesting that Sen. Paul is accusing us of having a "Gimme, gimme, gimme" attitude toward federal spending when in fact New Jersey is a donor state and we get 61 cents back on every dollar we send to Washington. Interestingly, Kentucky gets $1.51

on every dollar they send to Washington."

Rand Paul's response to this accusation is that some of the federal money goes to military bases in Kentucky and what should he do, "…shut down military bases in Kentucky?" Paul asked.

Well, there are two problems with Rand Paul's response. One, even if some of the federal funds go to the military bases, these same military bases generate enormous amounts of economic activity in his state. These military bases enable business to open where they are located – restaurants, fast food joints, grocery stores, homes, all kinds of retail activity etc. In fact, whole towns grow and thrive around military bases. All of which not only provide employment but also contribute to the state's coffers in taxes and contribute to the federal revenue from Kentucky.

For eg: let's say his state contributes $100 in taxes to the Fed. And lets say they receive $120 in spending funds from the Fed. This would result in Kentucky being a net "taker". But, according to Rand Paul, about $40 of the $120 funds from Fed goes to military bases, the actual Federal funding to his state is only $80 and thus his state is not a net taker but a net maker.

This is fine and dandy. But, he cannot on one hand say we should exclude the federal funds coming into this state that fund military bases, but on the other hand include the economic activity the same federal money generates on the revenue side. For instance, some of the contribution to the Federal revenue from Kentucky resulted from the economic activity **because** of the military bases. So, if one reduces the federal funding by $40 (from our example above) one also must reduce the revenue contribution as a result of the military bases. If one did that, I bet Kentucky will remain as a net "taker" state.

After the 2012 election, this taker v/s maker rhetoric from the conservatives was on the rise again with some of them suggesting that one of the reason why Obama got elected was because of the "welfare moms" and "food stamps dads" wanted to elect their "sugar daddy" so he keeps funneling money to these takers.

I am sure the liberals will gladly point out that in 2004 George W may have won because the "tax break dads" and "tax loophole business" wanted to elect their "sugar daddy" so he keeps funneling tax cuts to these takers.

If one actually looks at the states that actually were won by Romney, most of them fall into the taker category and a majority of states won by Obama fall into the maker category.

In an article "How the "Takers" voted", Stephanie Kelton put together an analysis that shows that, "…President Obama won 26 states plus the District of Columbia. Mitt Romney won 24 states. Of the 27 regions that were won by President Obama, seven (or 26%) are net recipients of fiscal transfers. Of the 24 states won by Mitt Romney, twenty (or 83%) are fiscal takers."

The following graph that appeared in this article tells it all. A vast majority of the states that voted Democratic are net "makers" whilst a majority of the states that voted Republican are net "takers".

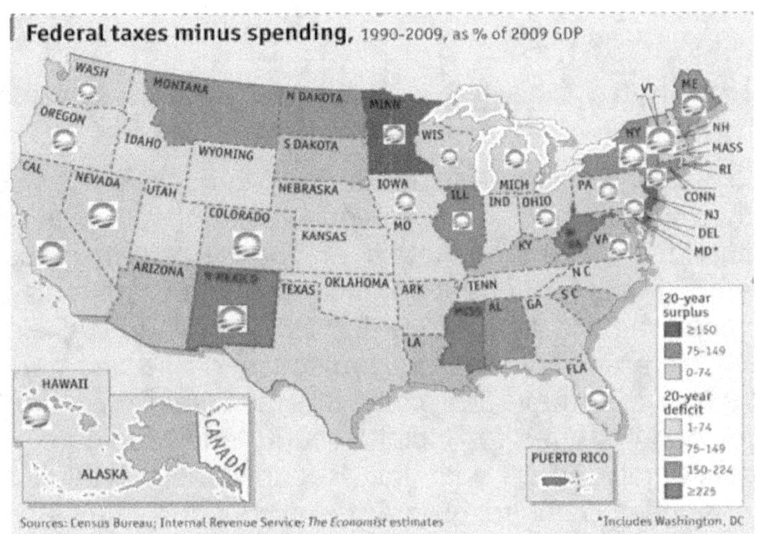

The alternate reality spin by the conservatives is completely bogus. If one really looks at the details and the real figures, the actual reality is that it is indeed most conservatives, even though they point at the other guy, are actually the takers.

Another Republican myth debunked!

Social Security, Medicare and Medicaid

I realize Social Security, Medicare and Medicaid do not conform to the theme of this book. However, I think these topics are very important in the greater context of budget reform discussions that are occurring (or should be occurring) at our nation's capitol. If you recall, before and during the 2012 presidential elections, Rep. Paul Ryan's plan was much discussed and debated about. Even though they have not come out and said it outright, their plan included changes to Social Security and Medicare. This is one point I fully agree with the Republicans - I think making some changes to these programs is critical if they are to be viable in the future. I may not agree completely with all the changes they are suggesting, but changes are needed. Thus, in this context I am including these topics here – not to de-bunk any Republican myth around these but to highlight the problems with these programs and how they get woven into the budget discussions.

As we have seen in the previous chapter, Social Security was created to provide economy security to the retired, the disabled, or families of retired, disabled or deceased workers. It does this by collecting taxes (FICA) from workers throughout their working period and pays out Social Security benefits once they retire or get disabled. Because of Social Security, it is estimated that over 40% of retirees over 65 years and above are out of poverty.

Medicare, the other program along with Social Security, provides retirees aged 65 years and above or the disabled or those with serious medical conditions, a federal health insurance program. The 2.9% of your income in taxes (half by you and half by your employer) paid throughout your working career pays for this benefit.

As we discussed before, most people do not think of Social Security and Medicare health insurance as entitlements. They view these as simply return on investments (contributions) they have been making throughout their working life. In this chapter we will look at how these programs are funded and payout and see whether or not the people get what they put in or more than what they put into these programs via contributions.

As also mentioned earlier, most people contribute to these through payroll taxes such as FICA (Social Security) at 12.4% (up to an income limit of $113,700 in 2013) and Medicare at 2.9%. The FICA and Medicare taxes are usually paid by employers and employees half and half. So, generally the employer pays 7.65% and the employee pays 7.65% up to the income limit. There is an upper income limit for Social Security, which in 2013 was $113,700, meaning any income above this number would not be taxed for FICA. There is no upper limit for the Medicare portion. Additionally, starting in 2013, anyone making more than $200,000 ($250,000 for a couple), had to pay 0.9% extra Medicare taxes.

The United States Social Security Administration collects payroll taxes and pays out the benefits by the use of "Trust Funds". There are two trust funds – the Old-Age and Survivors Insurance (OASI) and Disability Insurance (DI). When the program runs a surplus, the excess funds are invested in the treasury bonds, which provide interest income. If the program runs into a deficit in any given year, the surplus funds are used to pay the beneficiaries.

Both these trust funds represent a legal obligation to the social security beneficiaries. Since these trust funds invest in the treasury bonds (exclusively), the investments they make become part of the overall public debt, which is known as "intra-government" debt. As of 2012, over $5-trillion of the $16-trillion national debt was due to the social security investments.

Social Security

As of 2012, the OASI trust fund reported contributions of $731-million and payments of $645-million with reserves of $2.6-trillion (see table below).

Old-Age and Survivors Insurance (in millions)				
Fiscal year	Total income	Total outgo	Net increase	Assets at end of fiscal year
2004	$556,523	$417,053	$139,470	$1,452,550
2005	599,992	436,919	163,073	1,615,623
2006	632,157	455,560	176,597	1,792,220
2007	663,376	488,553	174,822	1,967,042
2008	692,873	509,864	183,009	2,150,052
2009	697,326	551,542	145,784	2,295,835
2010	682,448	579,907	102,541	2,398,377
2011	692,510	599,232	93,278	2,491,654
2012	728,981	634,700	94,281	2,585,936

Let's take an example and see how the social security numbers work on an individual basis. For this scenario, let's assume an individual named Bob earns $50,000 per year. He started working at age 25 and retired at age 65. And let's say he has been earning the same amount - $50K - for the 40-years of his work life. Note: we are using rough estimates here…. obviously, if someone starts with earning $50K would end up earning more at retirement. Alternately, if one is earning $50K at retirement, they may have started much lower when they first started. But, for this scenario, to keep things simple, we are assuming a $50K income all the way through.

His contributions to Social Security via FICA will be 12.4% of his salary, half paid by him and half paid by his employer. So, every year he contributes $6,200 into the Social Security fund. Over 40-years he would have contributed $248.000. When he retires at 65, he decides to take his social security benefits. Based on what he contributed and his age (and other factors), he qualifies to get $2,100 per month. This means he would draw down his contribution in about 10 years. And if he lives beyond the age 75, anything he gets from social security is above and beyond what he contributed. In other words, had he simply put his money in a bank account, he would have had $248,000 when he retired and he could draw down $2,100 each month for about 10-years until his account dries up.

Now, the above scenario assumes he did not earn any interest for the money he contributed. Let's assume he earned a modest 3% interest throughout the 40-year span. His total contributions would then increase to about $481,000 assuming his interest is compounded every month as his contributions are paid once a month (employers may be required to deposit tax payments with the IRS every payday). Now he can draw down his contributions for 19 years, until he is 84 years old. If he lives beyond 84-years, any benefits he gets from social security are a bonus.

Two points to consider here – one, we used a 3.8% interest rate that might seem high considering where the interest rates are today. But, in actuality this is the average interest rate reported by the Social Security Administration since some of the treasury bonds it holds actually pay more than 6% interest rate. Point Two, we used a straight-line 50K per year earnings over 40 years which is not a typical scenario.

In any case, under our scenario, this individual did not get any extra benefits from the government for 19 years – he was able to get the benefits for 19-years by simply drawing down what he contributed. Now, if he lived beyond 84-years, any benefit he gets is coming from other taxpayers.

So, in a nutshell, Social Security was designed to be self-sufficient. It was supposed to pay out the benefits from the contributions made by individuals via payroll taxes (or contributions from other individuals). And it was also designed to pay out less than what was being contributed to maintain excess balances as a rainy day fund. But over the past decades, several problems occurred.

One, people are living a lot longer than they used to when this program was created back in the 1960's. It is quite common to see people living well into their 80's and 90's. Therefore, they are beginning to (or will soon) exhaust their contribution (as in our scenario above) and go into deficit benefits (i.e. receiving more than their contributions).

Secondly, the Social Security Administration is required by law to only invest in treasury bonds. And as we know the interest rates for the past decade or so have been abysmal. Back in the 80's when the interest rates were at 10%-12%, there was plenty of interest income coming into the fund. With the current Trust Fund investments that mature far into the future (2020 and beyond) and pay below 2% interest, the income from interest will be greatly reduced for many years to come (see chart below).

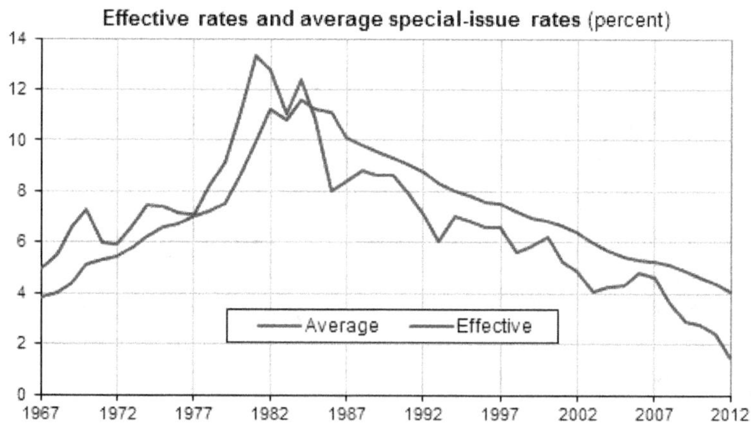

Thirdly, due to the deep recession and the prolonged recovery, a lot of people are still unemployed and thus are not contributing to the system. As you can see from the table below, the contributions into social security have reduced significantly over the past few years, especially in 2009 when the contributions were flat and in 2010 when they were actually under 3%. This is actually a triple whammy. When people retire two things happen – one, they collect social security benefits (i.e.: they drawdown) and two, they are not paying into the fund. So, the effect is quite significant. If we use our scenario above, the contributions of $6,200 per year are not coming in and the individual is getting benefits of $2,100 per month. So, the negative effect per year is $31,400 (6,200 + 2,100 x 12months). That's the double whammy. The third whammy is that because of the recession, the younger generation are having a tough time in finding jobs and therefore are not contributing into the system.

Year	Recepits Incr/Decr	Year	Recepits Incr/Decr
2001	6%	2007	5%
2002	4%	2008	3%
2003	1%	2009	0%
2004	4%	2010	-3%
2005	7%	2011	3%
2006	6%	2012	5%

Lastly, over the next decade or so, a lot of baby boomers will reach their retirement age and will start to draw down on their benefits. But, there is not a significant increase in the younger generation coming into the pool to offset the benefits that will be paid to the new retirees. This is either because the younger generation is limited in numbers (due to declining population growth) or the younger generation is earning lower wages, which reduces the taxes receipts. For eg: if a majority of the younger generation is earning $30K per year, their contribution into the Social Security pool will be 15% of $30k – about $4.5K per year. Whereas, if this new generation was earning $75K per year, their contribution would be 15% of $75K – about $11.2K per person.

Therefore, as we have stated in a previous chapter, it is imperative this younger generation is properly educated (college degree or technical diplomas) so they can compete for higher paying jobs. It is not only essential for them but also essential to maintain the retiring pool of seniors getting benefits from social security.

Disability Insurance

The second component of Social Security is the Disability Insurance. This is currently already in deficit since 2009 and is expected to get worse in the future (see the chart below - data from Social Security Administration site)

Disability Insurance (in millions)				
Fiscal year	Total income	Total outgo	Net increase	Assets at end of fiscal year
2004	$90,105	$78,471	$11,634	$182,893
2005	96,765	86,360	10,405	193,298
2006	101,571	92,932	8,640	201,938
2007	108,396	96,758	11,638	213,577
2008	109,816	107,153	2,663	216,239
2009	109,681	118,144	-8,462	207,777
2010	105,513	126,344	-20,831	186,946
2011	106,225	131,489	-25,264	161,682
2012	108,845	138,546	-29,701	131,981

Over the past two decades, the number of Americans claiming disability benefits more than doubled – from 5.2-million to 11.7-million. There are many reasons why the disability numbers are going up. The main one obviously is that as the population ages, the chances are higher they may become disabled.

But, there is a lot of fraud and abuse in the system as well. Some of the increases in disability numbers have nothing to do with a declining health of Americans; rather, it is mostly due to the fundamental flaws in the Social Security Disability Insurance (SSDI) administration process which by relaxing the eligibility criteria have made this into a long term unemployment program rather than a program of last resort for those unable to work due to their health. It's no coincidence that applications for disability go up during recessions or when unemployment is high.

Another issue that contributed to this growth in SSDI was the welfare reform enacted by President Clinton in the 90's. Part of President Clinton's reform required states to move people off welfare to work by making states pay a higher share of the welfare costs.   This "you-pay-more-if you-don't" motivation seemed to have worked. The states shrank their welfare rolls. But, the path from welfare to work was not a straight line. It took a by-pass into disability.   See the graphs below which point to this problem.

As the welfare rolls went down...

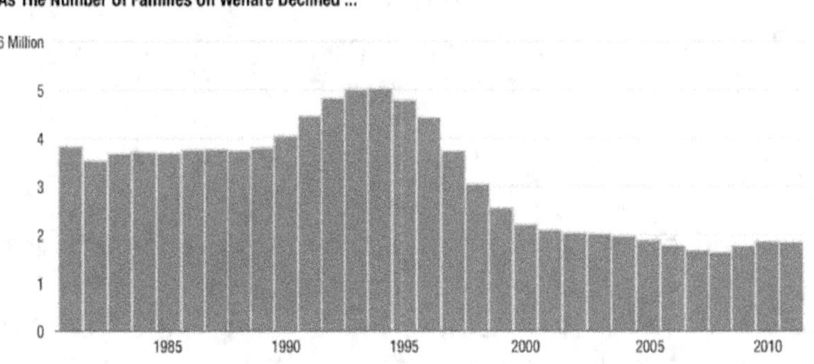

The Disability numbers went up…

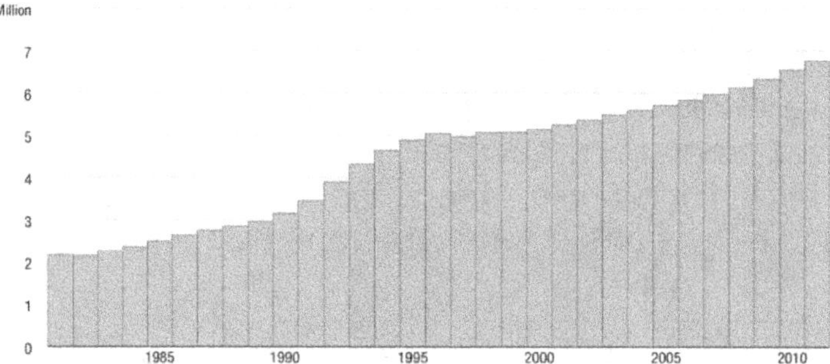

In addition, in 2004, the SSDI, facing a massive backlog of cases that not only prevented Americans from receiving benefits but also clogged up the court system, relaxed some of its regulations and allowed for non-lawyer experts to help clients fight their cases. If a disability case is won in a court, the people representing the case get a significant percent of the back-pay which is paid by SSDI. Many lawyers jumped into this massive loophole and made tons of money. And of course, since they only get paid if they win, they have an incentive to withhold critical information from the courts, which may have resulted in denial of benefits to their clients. The payments to lawyers went from $425-million in 2001 to $1.4-billion in 2010.

And this is not the only problem. In fact, when the case is heard in court, there is no one representing SSDI at the hearing. It's the client, their attorney and the judge. So, in these courtrooms, it's up to the judge to represent the government and make an objective determination. Since there is no one to challenge anything that is said and presented, many times the judges simply rubber stamp these cases as they are eager to move on to other backlogged cases. In fact, these lawyers usually file these cases in courts that have massive backlogs and in which they know the judge is lenient.

The problem is even worse than this. A story on NPR's This

<u>American Life reported in March 2013</u>, highlight a trend that is going on in some of the Republican states which are moving people from welfare into SDDI because, "…"A person on welfare costs a state money. That same resident on disability doesn't cost the state a cent, because the federal government covers the entire bill for people on disability. So states can save money by shifting people from welfare to disability."

These states hire companies like Public Consulting Group (PCG), which "..is a private company that states pay to comb their welfare rolls and move as many people as possible onto disability. "What we're offering is to work to identify those folks who have the highest likelihood of meeting disability criteria," Pat Coakley, who runs PCG's Social Security Advocacy Management team..."

And guess what? The state pays PCG every time it moves someone off of welfare and onto disability. PCG can get as much as $2,300 per person for moving them from welfare to disability. For states like Missouri, this is a deal – "…every time someone goes on disability, it means Missouri no longer has to send them cash payments every month. For the nation as a whole, it means one more person added to the disability rolls."

So, we not only have fraud and abuse in the SSDI system, but we also have states (mostly Republican) actively moving people off welfare to SSDI so they don't have to pay the welfare benefits. And these same Republicans complain that Obama is at fault for increasing the SSDI rolls.

The <u>chart</u> below gives a good perception on this problem. The national average of percent of population on SSDI is about 4.6%. The states where the percent is higher are all Republican states except for Michigan.

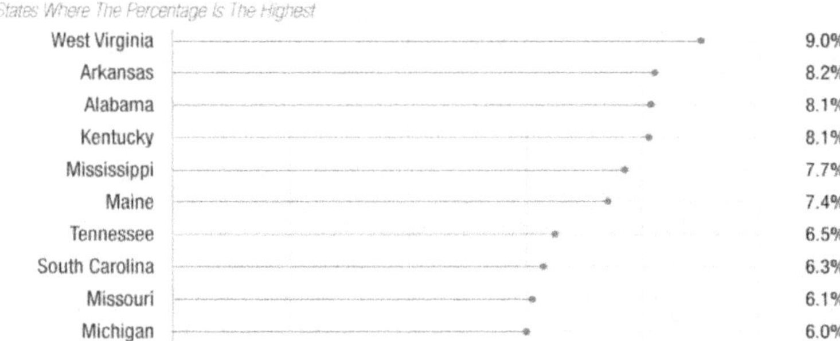

Medicare

Medicare is the second component of the social insurance program and as stated before, is paid for by the employees and their employers. Even self-employed people have to pay into the program. 2.9% of the earnings are targeted into Medicare contributions. But, unlike social security, there is no cap on the income for Medicare taxes – one has to pay 2.9% in taxes up to the full extent of your earnings. In addition, anyone earning more that $200,000 a year ($250,000 for a couple) has to pay an additional 0.9% in Medicare taxes.

The Medicare payroll taxes only cover Medicare Part "A" premiums that only cover hospitalization. The premiums for Medicare Part "B", that covers doctor's visits are taken out of Social Security Benefits payments. Most people pay a premium for this coverage which is about $100/month.

For about 49 million older and disabled Americans, Medicare is a lifeline. It helps pay for care in hospitals, nursing homes, outpatient clinics, doctors' offices, hospices and at home, as well as for prescription drugs.

But, the problem with Medicare is that it already costs too much.

In 2011, Medicare paid over $560billion in benefits. Unlike Social Security, Medicare contributions are only 2.9% of earned income. The total contributions by individuals as a result usually account for a small percent of the benefits they receive, especially given that the medical costs are skyrocketing. Using our case study from earlier, if a person makes $50,000 per year, total contributions to Medicare between them and their employer is $1,450 per year.

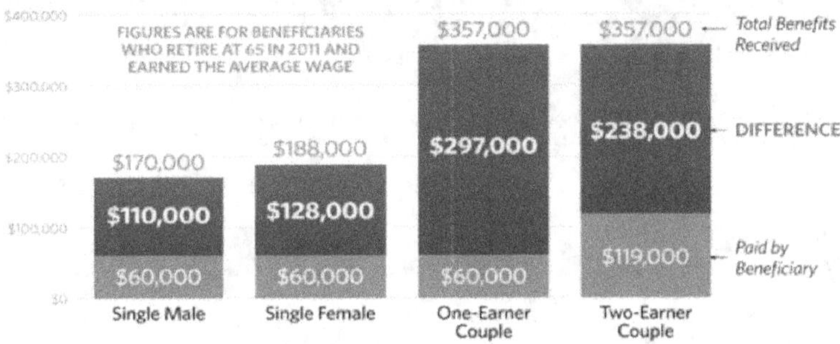

As you can see from the graph above (from www.heritage.org), there is a huge difference between what is contributed to what Medicare actually pays out. Many people believe that they pay for their own Medicare benefits (via payroll contributions), but in fact, most Medicare beneficiaries end up receiving more than what they paid into the system.

And the payments from Medicare are the fastest growing than all other entitlements (see chart below) when compared to 2002 to 2012.

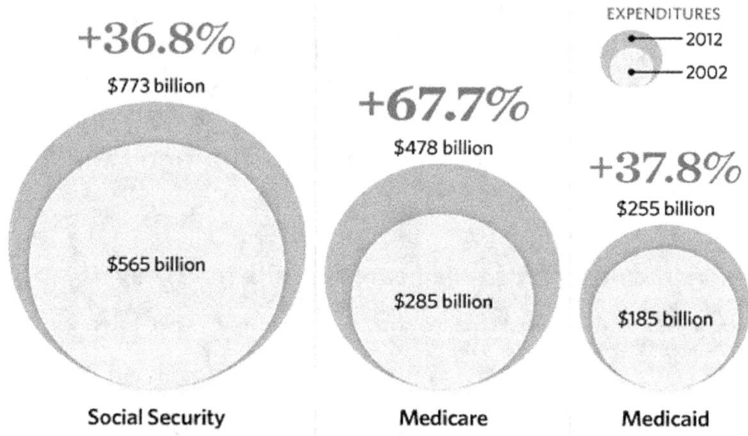

So, why are the costs going out of control? Three primary reasons.

Reason one: Demographic changes. Similar to the situation we discussed in the Social Security section, Medicare spending is projected to grow significantly over the next 25 years as the aging baby boomers enroll in the Medicare program. It is anticipated over 77 million baby boomers will become eligible in the next 2 decades which will raise the Medicare participants from 50-million to 81-million by 2030 (see chart below).

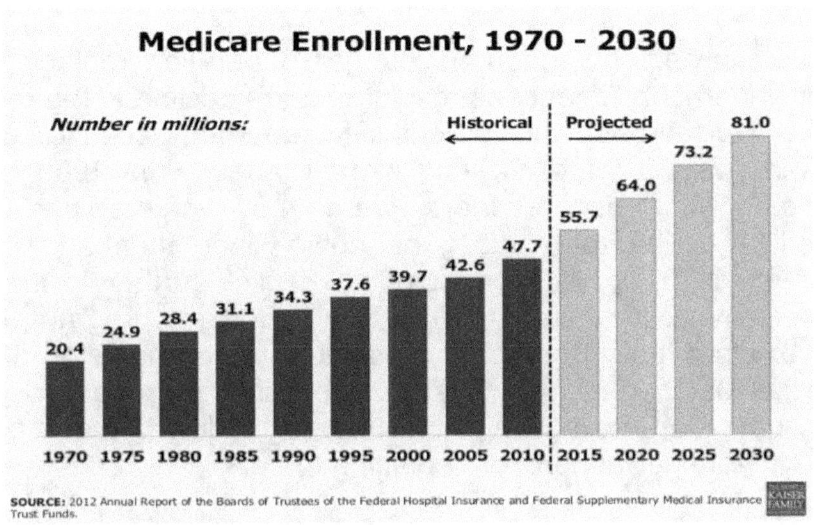

Reason two: people are living longer. The average life expectancy when Medicare was created was around 70 years. Which meant on average, Medicare paid the benefits for 5 years after someone retired at 65. The life expectancy today is around 75 years and is supposed to be around 80 years by 2020. This means most of the baby boomers retiring will draw benefits from Medicare for over 15 years stressing the Medicare program even more.

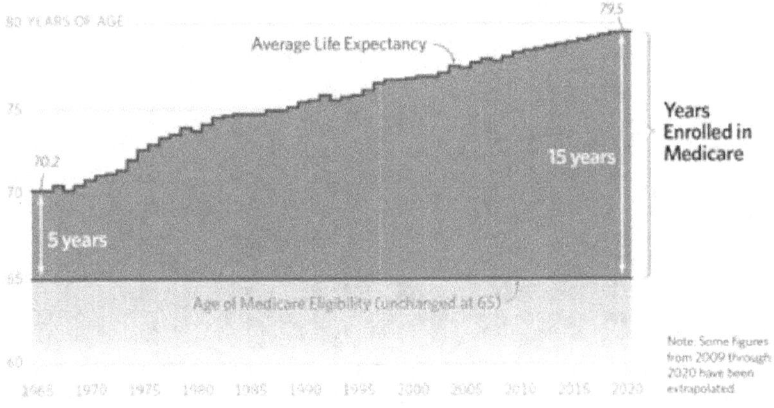

Reason three: not enough younger generation replacing the older generation Americans resulting in the decline in the ratio of workers to retirees, which is critically important because current workers pay for the existing beneficiaries. In 1965 when Medicare first began, there were 4.5 workers per each beneficiary. The ratio has gone down since then and is 3.3 workers in 2011. It is projected to decline further to just 2.3 workers by 2030. Similar to the Social Security program, there also exists a triple whammy. As seniors retire, they stop paying into the Medicare program (since they are no longer working), and they start collecting benefits. In addition, there is not enough younger generation replacing them.

Social Security, Disability Insurance and Medicare are three programs that need to be fixed if they are to be viable long term. And of course, there is a wide gap between how democrats want to fix this and how republicans want to fix this.

Conclusion

Over several chapters we have looked at the detailed figures and have determined that most of the rhetoric and narrative from the Republicans and conservatives is nonsense and nothing but spin.   Despite what their rhetoric says and despite what the perception is, the facts are clear. Democrats do a better job at creating jobs, better job at deficit reduction, better job at debt reduction, better job at contributing to the federal revenues and better job at education, better job at taking care of the poor and the unfortunate and better at providing equal opportunity and better at fairness.

Having said this, there are many things the Democrats can do better. For eg: the "welfare" system does need fixing. There is indeed a growing reliance on the welfare system by some people and there is indeed fraud in the system. Some people scam the system by finding loopholes and some become dependent on it. And this trend is increasing.

But it is worthwhile to note that fraud is everywhere and not just in the welfare system. As we have seen recently, a lot of people got scammed on Wall Street, scammed in the mortgage industry, scammed in the banking industry and of course who can forget Bernie Madoff who swindled billions from innocent investors. But, if you noticed, none of the tea-partiers or the conservatives have called for regulations and controls over Wall Street and the banks. In fact, they still champion less regulation for Wall Street and Banks. But, for some reason, they are laser focused on the scamming that occurs in the welfare system - almost to a point of obsession.

The education system must be fixed to encourage higher education including technical education and training so people with high school diplomas have a path to better jobs or even to find jobs. For instance, the focus should shift to educating and training people in jobs that cannot be outsourced – eg: medical technicians, auto-repair, HVAC repair, mechanical systems repairs & maintenance etc, or, helping high school graduates in pursuing degrees in STEM fields. In fact, Obama recognized the need to improve our graduation rates in STEM fields and he announced a goal of 1-million STEM graduates in 10-years. Here's an idea. Why not offer free-college tuition to anyone pursuing STEM degrees with a requirement that they should do some volunteering after they graduate or some such requirement. I will bet this will encourage a lot of people to pursue STEM degrees and get us globally competitive again.

As far as the economy is concerned, now that it is on the right track again, I hope Obama and the Democrats in Congress get off their behind and start focusing on reducing spending and the debt. I understand the priority in 2009 and 2010 was to get the economy going again. Reducing the deficit was not the right time then – but it is the right time now.

As far as the conservative rhetoric is concerned, we have to give them credit – they are masters of spin! They have developed the spin into such an art form that most of us don't even realize it. They have elevated the tactics of rhetoric and propaganda to such a high level, most of the conservatives and independents and even some liberals believe it without question. Most of the conservatives don't even realize the hypocrisy that is inherent in their actions.

I came across the following comments in a blog, which I think explains this phenomenon. Unfortunately, I don't seem to recall which blog so I cannot give proper credit to this individual.

> On a general note regarding "takers" and "makers," they way I see it, people who whine about "big government" are those who are resent it when other people (in addition to themselves) benefit from government spending. If I am a cut-the-deficit Tea Party type, and government spending promotes my personal views and values, and benefits me at the expense of others, then (for me) the government is great. But if other people benefit from government spending in addition to me, then government is "bad." It is "bug government."
>
> For right-wingers, massive government spending on war and the military industrial complex is proper and good. Everything else is support for "welfare queens."
>
> For Wall Street types, massive government bailouts that benefit rich financiers is "efficient" and "patriotic." All other government spending is "anti-market."
>
> If I am a Tea Party-type who relies on food stamps, then I "deserve" food stamps. The government "owes" them to me. Meanwhile I regard unwed mothers who receive government assistance for medical care to be "parasites."
>
> I see this same phenomenon even among Libertarians. If government does what they want it to do, this is "liberty." If other people have different ideas about what government should do, this is "tyranny."

I don't believe I could have said it any better.

As we also have seen both parties – the Democrats and the Republicans – have contributed to the problems faced by our nation. From racking up massive debt to the unsustainable "welfare" system to the unsustainable tax structures, both the parties are equally responsible for it. Therefore, the only way we can fix our problems is for both these parties to accept responsibility and stop the mud slinging at each other and work together for the greater good of the country.

The new found emphasis and attitude on what's in it for me and how can I get rich even at the expense of others will ultimately have a long term impact on our nation. Instead of "me, me, me" nation, we must start thinking about what is good for the nation in general. We must start thinking about what is good for our country and for our society rather than just me as an individual. Likewise, our politicians must get back to acting in terms of what is good for the country and the world and not just what is good for themselves and their party.

And more importantly, we the people need to take responsibility and ask the right questions and get the facts for ourselves and then decide for ourselves who is telling the truth. Blindly believing the rhetoric and subjecting ourselves to be brainwashed will continue to embolden the politicians on both sides and only make matters worse.

----------End---------